IMAGES OF THE UNTOUCHED

Images of the Untouched

Virginity in Psyche, Myth and Community

edited by

Joanne Stroud and Gail Thomas

THE PEGASUS FOUNDATION SERIES I

published for

The Dallas Institute of Humanities and Culture

DALLAS, TEXAS

by Spring Publications, Inc.

ACKNOWLEDGMENTS

Acknowledgments for quotations from other works have been made in the appropriate places in the text. John Layard's essay was first published in the *Eranos Jahrbücher,* Volume XII/1945, and later included in *The Virgin Archetype,* Spring Publications, 1972, 1977.

The cover image is adapted from a photograph of the "Bust of a Young Girl," Andrea della Robbia, Bargello Museum, Florence.

The Pegasus series, sponsored by the Pegasus Foundation, publishes books and monographs concerned with the imaginative, mythic, and symbolic sources of culture. Publication efforts are centered at the Dallas Institute of Humanities and Culture. Many of the works in the series result from seminars and conferences of the Institute devoted to the application of mythic-symbolic imagination to critical issues of contemporary culture.

Produced at Open Studio in Rhinebeck, New York, a non-profit facility for independent publishers and individual artists, funded in part by grants from the New York Council on the Arts & the National Endowment for the Arts.

European agent: Spring, Postfach, 8800-Thalwil, Switzerland.
Japanese agent: Japan Spring Sha, Inc.
31, Shichiku-Momonomoto-Cho
Kitaku, Kyoto 603 Japan

ISBN: 0-88214-317-4
LCCN: 81-84496

LCCN Information:
Lopez-Pedraza, Rafael et al
Images of the Untouched.

Dallas: Spring Publications
184 p.
8111 810921

CONTENTS

Editors' Preface

Virginity rarely allows close contact. A first attempt to get close to this image, however, was made in February 1979 at a conference in Dallas sponsored by the journal *Dragonflies* edited by Robert Sardello. Six of the eight essays in this volume were read at the conference; in addition, Dr. Miller and Dr. Sardello were invited to submit articles which have been included in this collection.

It seems important to amplify the realm of the virgin, for we are all pulled by the virgin's lure. Why is it so compelling? Where in our daily lives are we psychic virgins? We feel ambivalence toward this complex image; demands of the virginal soul, 'to have one's own space' or 'not to come too close' seem to appear with double meaning: they provide valuable topographical clues for familiarity with one's own individual nature, and yet they sever, cut, isolate, and reject in such a way as to threaten life-sustaining relationships. The eight essays of this collection attempt to explore these virginal demands in greater detail.

Mary Helen Gray supervised the book's production. Doug Gerwin served as manuscript editor, Dana Anderson as copy editor. The cover was designed by Kate Smith Passy. We express to them our gratitude.

Joanne Stroud and Gail Thomas

Foreword

Joanne Stroud

> "To speak on the part of virginity is to accuse your mothers, which is most infallible disobedience. He that hangs himself is a virgin: virginity murders itself, and should be buried in highways, out of all sanctified limit, as a desperate offendress against nature. Virginity breeds mites, much like a cheese, consumes itself to the very paring, and so dies with feeding his own stomach. Besides, virginity is peevish, proud, idle, made of self-love, which is the most inhibited sin in the canon." Parolles: *All's Well That Ends Well* I:i, 150-159.

When we encounter an image which touches us — which awakens the imagination, stirs the instincts, alerts the psyche — we may conclude that we are confronting a phenomenon essentially paradoxical, by definition ambiguous. The image of the virgin recurs throughout the history of literature, mythology, and art — all forms by which man has tried to embody himself in the language of the psyche. In an attempt to plumb the potentialities and power of the virgin image, its diverse meanings, including its traditional religious context, a group of scholars from the disciplines of mythology, psychology, theology, comparative religious studies, and literature assembled in Dallas in February, 1979 for a conference under the auspices of the journal *Dragonflies: Studies in Imaginal Psychology*. Out of the papers presented at this conference, and from subsequent exchanges of ideas, there arose a new appreciation of the power of this complex and at times disturbing image. That appreciation forms the contents of this book.

To those accustomed to the androgynous nature of foundational archetypes it will come as no surprise that the image of the virgin reflects aspects of the psyche of males no less than of females. On a personal level, the virgin mode manifests itself in one's search for solitude, in the desire to keep distance, remain uninvolved (in contrast to other modes which would draw one into relationship, connection, engagement). We are in the grip of the virgin in those moments when we cut the first path of the ski trail on a virginally crystalline morning, or when we sip cold water from a pure stream in the wilderness. The same appeal underlies our desire to protect the virginal lands of Alaska, to leave part of our nation untouched.

The image of the virgin evokes that which is chaste, pure, holy, undefiled: the perfect receptacle for the son of God. And yet with the characteristic perversity of archetypes, the virgin, too, has a shadowy, dark, chthonic depth, more difficult to recover. This darker side of the image can be sensed when we probe beyond the immediate loveliness of Della Robbia's *Bust of a Young Girl* (whose averted look will have drawn your attention on our cover). Giorgioni's *The Sleeping Venus* depicts the goddess reclining naked on a white cloth, her eyes closed. How different this Renaissance painting would be were her eyes open! She might then appear the brazen "hussy" described by Homer. Instead, sleep lends innocence. In the act of sleeping—that state of total passivity, helplessness, oblivion—even promiscuous Venus appears untouchably innocent.

The occasional epithet describing the virgin as "the unawakened" reinforces the connection between virginity and slumber. She is self-enclosed and remote, living in a world of seclusion, turning an inward rather than an outward face to the world. Tom Moore, connecting her with the unicorn, explains: "The virgin tends to put a lock on her 'enclosed garden,' a kind of chastity belt of the imagination which keeps one distant from the vitality, as well as the pain of Dionysian Life."

In her guise of unawakened maid, the virgin may express icy aloofness, the defensiveness of one untouched by those sexual yearnings which would rupture the shell of self-sufficiency. Exclusive, solitary, and complete unto herself, she may live by Parolles's dictum: "Virginity is peevish, proud, idle, made of self-love, which is the most inhibited sin in the canon." She may allow only spirit to enter her enchanted circle of awareness, while excluding instinct, holding herself chaste in narcissistic self-love. Alternatively, the virgin may induce us to remain in the realm of the fantastical (as distinguished from the imaginal) where in the words of Patricia Berry, "the psyche is still virginal as though fascinated with its own frivolousness."

The image which speaks or connects in any profound way is a container for dualities. The virginal attitude allows us a sense of being one-with-ourselves. It imparts that sense of selfhood which frees us from conforming or adapting merely in order to please other people. In sensing self as worthy of upholding, we act under the aegis of the virgin, maintaining the mode of self-enclosure against the demands of convention or abstract opinion.

To understand virginity merely as a biological fact is to literalize and thereby lose some of its potential meanings. The archetype of the virgin is operative in masculine figures, too. Rafael Lopez-Pedraza, in his essay "Moon Madness – Titanic Love," relates masculine virginity to the inner excess of Endymion, "the one who finds himself within." His loyal love for the moon goddess Selene confines him to "a cave asleep with his eyes open." He is "untouched by other possibilities in life." The image of the moon – reflected light personified in the figures of Selene or Diana – also magnifies our perspective of the image. David Miller, in his article "Womb of Gold, Body of the Sun," likens the Virgin Mary to the moon, reflecting the light of the Christ sun.

Today we often tend to define the virginal by collapsing its multiple implications into a single image. The ancient Greeks, by contrast, captured the polymorphous possibilities which any archetype can manifest. The varied modes of womanhood were expressed in terms of the most significant goddesses:

> Among the ladies of Mount Olympus, Hera, Athene, Artemis, and Aphrodite are supreme. We might divide them into two groups: Hera and Aphrodite representing woman in her capacity as mother and loved one; Artemis and Athene typifying the virgin, one lonely and close to nature, the other intellectual and active in the community. It may fairly be said that these four women signalize the four aspects of all womanhood.[1]

It is curious that Greek thought distinguishes the functions of virgin and mother so thoroughly. When Athene is called *mother* it is a term which designates her as progenitor of an institution rather than of a child.

In the Christian tradition the two aspects of femininity are intimately combined in the person of the Virgin-Mother. As Tom Carroll suggests, "it is important to note in the patristic tradition the Virgin-Mother image is never divided. Mary is never just Virgin or just the Mother: likewise the Church is never one at the expense of the other."

For the Greeks, the virgin goddesses express alternative modes of relating: Artemis is aloof, Athene close to the scene of action:

> In Artemis maidenhood has a tart, shy, disdaining character which fends love off; in Athena, maidenhood is the spirit of action. It is her nature to associate with men, to think of them always, always to be near them, in order to reveal herself to them in moments of life which differ from the erotic not by shy aloofness but by the strength and clarity of energetic action.[2]

Artemis wanders alone or with a stag in the woods. Surrounded by "the hallowed solitude of untouched nature," she mirrors "free nature with its brilliance and wildness, with its guiltless purity and its uncanniness."[3] The virginity of Artemis evokes that which is remote, wild, untrammeled in nature, the purity of the untouched. "In the classical figure of this goddess, the wildness and the terrors meet at a border-line: they are in equilibrium."[4] William B. Yeats likens this appeal of the virgin wild to the call of the Muses:

> Seek those images
> That constitute the wild,
> The lion and the virgin,
> The harlot and the child,
>
> Find in middle air
> An eagle on the wing,
> Recognize the five
> That make the Muses sing?

Being true to one's virginal call can keep one aloof from the mass of commonplace opinion — listening instead to one's own personal muse, or remaining simply aloof.

Like Artemis, the virgin may be solitary, somewhat disdainful of men; or, like Athene, she may operate in close proximity to the male, though always in the role of sister or *inspiratrix*. The masculinity with which the virgin interacts is not necessarily always external. Hostilities and amiabilities are constantly changing place, sometimes external and sometimes internal. The virginal feminine aspects of a person may be in close or in remote juxtaposition to the masculine within, imparting courage to our action or causing us to run from action.

Athene and Artemis are united, it is true, by a common opposition to the complications of Aphrodite. *The Homeric Hymns* to the goddess of love acknowledge Aphrodite's supremacy over all mortals and immortals, even Zeus; but her power dissolves before Athene and Artemis. Although she does not succumb to erotic love, Artemis can in other ways exercise an irresistible power of attraction. Louise Cowan, in her essay on William Faulkner's theme of "non-consummation," of not seizing that which one has the opportunity to seize, says that "part of the anguish experienced in the yearning for Artemis stems from the fact that, as Karl Kerényi points out, her maidenhood, unlike that of Athene, is not absolute. She is attainable. Athene's maidenhood excludes the very possibility of her succumbing to a man; with Artemis on the other hand, her maidenhood presupposes this possibility." Artemis, "whose sweet strangeness draws man on the more irresistibly the more disdainfully it dismisses him,"[5] has unmistakable, though ambivalent, magnetism. Her message is double: she both attracts the male and repels his advances. Ovid relates the tale of Actaeon — both drawn on and destroyed by the same image. The virgin punishes when one oversteps the boundaries of connectedness or becomes over-possessive.

Artemis calls to mind another mythological maiden, Persephone, "whose salient feature was an *elemental virginity*."[6] Homer calls both virgins *hagne*: "holy" or "pure." "Persephone was exempt from the passions which swayed other divinities."[7] Her lack of Eros invites opposition, just as the purity of Hippolytus' devotion to Artemis invites Aphrodite's ire. Does the virginal attitude constitute a movement leading away from the earthiness of body or is it an emergence of spirit antithetical to the body? In discussing the Demeter-Persephone bond, Robert Sardello argues that "the action of virginizing intensifies the sensing body. We cannot look upon transformation of the bond with the earth to the bond with the soul as one which leaves the body behind." Rejection of the body always courts revenge.

Artemis and Persephone both exemplify a figure who may simultaneously seek to repel and attract the attacker. Somehow the very posture of exclusiveness constellates aggression, since "the consummation of virginity lies in its 'desecration.' "[8] The Demeter-Persephone experience is a narrow circle "which is alien to man and shuts him out,"[9] a posture which challenges the seducer or conqueror. Persephone personifies the archetypal image of the virgin who is sexually assaulted: she is passive before the advances of Hades. Facing one's depths alone and feeling defenseless against the onslaught of the shadowy underworld: such is the virginal state of *pathos* or passivity.

To become fixated on the image of the virgin is comparable to looking into an abyss that opens up rather as the earth gapes before Persephone: like her we are drawn into death or ghost-like existence. If we attempt to hold back time, to remain in virginal time, we court a shocking awareness of mortality. The virginal endures a unique relationship to life and growth. The radical denial of fertility and fecundity conceals the underlying demand that time stand still. Virgins sacrifice growth and maturity at the altar of eternal youth: "We are each virginal when we are preserved from experience," says James Hillman in his essay on "Salt: A Chapter in Alchemical Psychology," which closes this collection. In this state, he maintains, "neither life nor insight is possible: only dedication, barren and pure."

These papers raise many of the forgotten faces of the virgin image. In their complexity and diversity, they suggest the infinite opportunities for continued exploration of the images of the untouched.

In a sense, we are still virginal in our perception of the virgin.

1. Bruno Snell, *The Discovery of the Mind* (New York: Harper and Row, 1960), p. 40.
2. Walter Otto, *The Homeric Gods*, trans. Moses Hadas (New York: American Book-Stratford Press, Inc., 1954), p. 54.
3. *Ibid.*, pp. 80-81.
4. C.G. Jung and Carl Kerényi, *Essays on a Science of Mythology*, Bollingen Series XXII (Princeton: Princeton University Press, 1971), p. 105.

5. *Ibid.*, p. 107.
6. *Ibid.*, p. 150.
7. *LaRousse Encyclopedia of Mythology* (London: Hamlyn Press, 1959), p. 165.
8. F.A.C. Wilson, *W.B. Yeats and Tradition* (London: Methuen and Co., 1968), p. 94.
9. Jung, "The Archetypes of the Collective Unconscious," in *Collected Works*, 9, trans. R.F.C. Hull, Bollingen Series XX (Princeton: Princeton University Press, 1959), § 383.

Moon Madness – Titanic Love
A Meeting of Pathology and Poetry

Rafael Lopez-Pedraza

For this paper, I borrow material from two of my works in progress. The central image with which we shall be concerned is the mad love of the mythological figure of Endymion and the Moon. The image belongs to a seminar which I am preparing on the Moon and is stimulated by images from the first Tier – Diana – of Giulio Camillo's Renaissance Memory Theatre. The mythology of Endymion has attracted many poets and writers,[1] but my aim is to make a connection between mythology (a concern of literature) and Archetypal Psychology; the mythologem of Endymion offers a field for exploring this kind of connection. Endymion is presented as being in love with the Moon as Selene, a Titaness, thus his psychological picture includes a Titanic side through this connection to the Moon, in the mythology of the archetypes – the virgin, the virginal untouched side of nature. So, first, I would like to share with you some impressions of Titanism and indicate its importance in my studies in Archetypal Psychology. For this purpose, I extract some of my ideas from another seminar – this one on the Titanic, which for me represents a very important and not fully explored side of man's nature.

There seems to have been no cult of the Titans. Titanic times can be viewed as a sort of transitional period between primitive man and cultured, civilized man, a period during which there was neither the ritual and cult of the primitive man nor the well-defined anthropomorphic imagery of the highly cultured and religious man. Now, just as we all have primitive complexes within us so well worked out by Jungian psychology, so we must all have, implicitly, a Titanic level of the psyche – Titanic complexes – though not so explicitly worked out. A more differentiated psychology at this Titanic level is still waiting to be tackled. There are personalities, too, in which the Titanic seems to predominate. And, as well, there are odd behaviors and pathologies which can only be evaluated in terms of Titanism, something I shall refer to in more detail later. I believe the psychology of the Titan is very important, particularly if we accept that the Titanic ingredient is in all of us.

First, let me clarify a bit the mythological field in which the image we shall be focusing on resides. But in order to clear the ground for a clearer idea of the Titanic, we need to take a look at what it is not. The Titans belong to the mythological time of Kronos, the time of the first and second generations of the Gods. This was the time before Zeus waged war on his Titanic progenitors and brought about a new order, ritual, religion, culture, and civilization. Zeus' new world also brought about a differentiation of images, what Nilsson calls the Greek anthropomorphism in mythology and history. Nilsson and other modern scholars agree that it took about a millenium to realize this anthropomorphism. During those hidden centuries of the Greek Dark Ages, it was the task of bards and minstrels – the poets, in other words – to sing the same songs over and over again, to repeat the Mycenaean heroic sagas: that is, the mythologized history of the Heroes. And as the poets sang, they wove a net which caught, little by little, the images of a divine mythology. Into this net of repeated tales they wove the Gods and Goddesses as living anthropomorphic images. This was how the clarity of the well-differentiated, *consistent* image was created. Moreover, as Nilsson states,

> during the Dark Ages between the fall of the Mycenaean culture and the Homeric period – the time when the specifically Greek anthropomorphism must have been developed – it is to be presumed that the *internal* anthropomorphism was the leading force.... For we have been educated by the Greeks to a consistent anthropomorphism and this is something specifically Greek.[2]

We, today, can be educated once again by the Greeks — the constant possibility of a Renaissance in the psyche. We have been educated by the Greeks; but, for the sake of precision, I would add, by the Greek *poets*. I consider this education to be an education of the soul. It is a psychical education. And this education of the soul through poetry — poetical, mythological anthropomorphism — is the reservoir from which Western man can draw to educate and make his soul again and again.[3]

Hölderlin wrote: "Full of merit, yet poetically man dwells on earth."[4] With this line, the poet tells us that our education today contains both what man does by merit and by poetical intervention. In order to reflect the image which I shall be elaborating, we shall also need merit and poetry.

But let us get back to the Titans. Unfortunately, we know very little about them. The *Titanomachia* and two-thirds of Aeschylus' trilogy on Prometheus were lost, but for our purposes here, scholars of mythology give us an adequate image of the ancient race of Gods. Here is what Kerényi has to say of the Titans:

> The stories of the Titans are about gods who belong to such a distant past that we know them only from tales of a particular kind, and only as exercising a particular function. The name of Titan has, since the most ancient times, been deeply associated with the divinity of the Sun, and seems originally to have been the supreme title of beings who were, indeed, celestial gods, but gods of very long ago, still savage and subject to no laws.[5]

Kerényi gives us a general picture of the psychology of the Titans: no laws, no order, no limits. In his extraordinary work on Prometheus, a Titan, Kerényi named him "the archetype of human existence,"[6] although he was careful to say that he wished to avoid the philosophical connotation of Existentialism in his use of the word "existence." However, it was his conception of Prometheus as the archetype of human existence, as well as what we see of Titanism under the magnifying glass in the works of some of the masters of modern literature, that sparked my insights into Titanism as it appears in our time. Kerényi, a great pioneer who made the connection between the excessiveness of the Titans and human existence, was undoubtedly, despite what he says, under the twofold influence of Jung's research on the archetypes and the ideas and literature inspired by Existentialism. These ideas, in a man who was a war exile, must have helped to make possible his *Prometheus*, a textbook study which introduces the difficult psychology of the Titans and which gave me a point of departure for my own reflections.[7]

For didactic purposes, we can say that, just as the Greeks thought of the Titanic times as the reign in earlier times of more savage celestial Gods, in the ontogenesis of man, there are Titanic times, too. Probably our adolescence contains a lot of Titanism – excess, unboundedness, lawlessness, chaos, barbarism, and so on. We can add this Titanic element to the Puer's celestial trip, which exhibits its own excessiveness, lack of limitation, and destructiveness.[8]

My own reflections of Titanism come out of the recollections of my own life, from living in Titanic societies which, psychologically, could be said to be sandwiched between primitive and civilized man; and, why not, from observing excess everywhere in today's life, even in the most differentiated societies whose traditions are based on the High Religion – an excess which is most evident in a missionary zeal predominating in all facets of life. Western civilization is becoming more and more Titanic. But, above all, my reflections come out of my practice, based upon patients whose psychology makes sense only if one can detect the Titanic element – what Jung and others might call simply shadow or unconscious – and appreciate how Titanic they are despite their most articulate and cultured self-expression in a way of speech that can, however, be heard as mimetic jargon.

For me, to be unconscious is to be unconscious of the archetypes, either in history or in a lifetime; to equate Titanism with the unconscious, then, is quite another business. For example, with these patients, the motto that I have adopted – "The image, what makes possible the impossible"[9] – simply does not work. To 'make possible' is to 'make conscious' an image that has been 'impossible.' These patients, however, are unable to make an image; or just when one thinks an image is in process, something coming out of nowhere destroys any such possibility. Sometimes, one can see that when they offer what could be called an image, there are no accompanying psychical feelings and no creativity coming out of that image; what one is taking as an image which could move psyche, is for them a stereotype, a mimetism. Another way of detecting Titanism is in what Jungian psychology has called 'the Intellectual.' There is an intellectual approach to the image, an approach one can see with a magnifying glass when a dream is only intellectualized.

(One wonders whether the method of amplification feeds intellectualism.) Let us push this Titanic element a bit further. Kerényi's view of the Titans, that they represent a particular function, is perhaps what I am trying to get at concerning this Titanic ingredient which we all have. However, we are faced here with a difficulty; a function points to something specific, whereas Titanism seems so messy and wild.

I have already mentioned the well-defined Gods and Goddesses with their *consistent* images; in other words, the archetypes. Nilsson again: "Anthropomorphism has, therefore, a characteristic *limitation*."[10] If that is so, it is difficult to see the Titans (whose main characteristic is excess) as archetypes with their own inherent limitation, and even more difficult to see them as the images of an archetype. Furthermore, Nilsson states: "The Titans are abstractions or empty names of whose significance we cannot judge."[11] So to call the Titans archetypes, or even as representatives of a particular function, is a bit risky.[12] Nevertheless, in poetry and iconography the Titans *are* personified, represented as forms, enabling us, perhaps, to broaden our view of anthropomorphism and imagine the forms of the Titans as a sort of borderline anthropomorphism. Personally, I prefer to view them as mythological *figures* representing mimicry and excess, for they are not archetypal configurations. In order to have insight into this mimetism, jargon, and excess, we need to have a strong archetypal training and point of view; it is only by having those well-defined forms as a background that we can have the insight into what is, by definition, formless in human nature.

Kerényi wrote *Prometheus* in 1946, just after the Second World War when, it seems, man began to be aware of hitherto unknown aspects of himself, as if the war had pushed him into reflecting on some estranged parts of himself. We have the literature running from Camus' *The Outsider*, published during the war in 1942, to Anthony Burgess' *A Clockwork Orange*, to confirm this impression.[13] I connect what Camus and Burgess brought in their novels, in terms of mythology and Archetypal Psychology, with the Titanic level in man which we have been tracking: no laws, no order, no limits—in short, excess. Once again, it is literature which has opened the door to an exploration (which we in psychology are just beginning) of those levels in man where the Titan lurks. But, following Kerényi again, we have to accept that, in the history of human life, the Titanic expresses itself where we are excessive. In this sense, the Titanic could be, if not an archetype, then a particular function.

Let me return to Nilsson's statement about the Titans whom, as you recall, he terms "abstractions or empty names of whose significance we cannot judge."[14] Careful thought about this statement offers us another point of reflection which helps to give us a wider view of Titanism. We are all inhabited by these abstractions, these empty names; we are flooded in our daily lives by empty names – our daily "blah-blah-blah" – not to mention our psychotherapy, in which, if we are unaware of our Titanism, we can fall into an empty jargon, even when using the most beautiful words. Our psychotherapy can become empty names – Titanic jargon. There are areas in our psyches, or in our lives, in which we have no reflection because there are no images and so no feelings to judge. Keeping in mind these two basic elements of Titanism – its emptiness on the one hand, its excess on the other – we can begin to evaluate excessiveness throughout our history, our life, and our practice. Our challenge is to bring reflection to that which has no limits, to that which is not archetypal, to that which, paradoxically, cannot be reflected because it has no images – though it can be detected through its own Titanic rhetoric.[15]

Now, Nilsson's statement that the Titans are "abstractions or empty names" enables us to push our inquiry in another direction, that of our so-called lacunae: that which we cannot know or grasp in ourselves, those empty abstractions, the nothings, the holes – those black holes which fascinate everyone just now. No archetypes, these, but holes. If we can hold both the emptiness and the excess, we are in a better position to be aware of the Titanic. Actually, the excess could come out of the emptiness, the lacunae.

This discussion of the Titans should, I hope, aid us in Archetypal Psychology to acquire a basic outlook of the field they offer for study. It would be a pity, after all, if Archetypal Psychology became no more than the study of the archetypes, merely depicting the characteristic profiles of Artemis, Aphrodite, Mars, and so on. Rather, the most important element of the Titan – the excess, which, as far as I can see, comes out of the emptiness – leads, among other things, into the psychopath or 'odd behavior': the excess that history and all of us are filled with.

I have leaned rather heavily on Kerényi and Nilsson, but, as far as I know, Kerényi was the first to approach Titanism in depth, and Nilsson's contribution adds tremendously to our insights. As you know, there is little mention of the Titans in Jungian psychology. What little there is has to do with the old Orphic Platonic connections between the Titans and the evil in human nature. As Dodds points out, "Plato, in his *Laws*, referred to people 'who show off the old Titan nature,' and to impulses which are 'neither of man nor of God' ":[16] that is to say, in Jungian terms, the evil in our shadow we cannot integrate and so have to reject. Certainly, Jungian psychology has not allowed modern literature and the imagery of our times to provide a reflection of this part of nature which is usually called 'existence,' and which I equate with Titanism.

I now return to Camus and Burgess. From the very first lines of *The Outsider*, we are given an extraordinary picture of *emptiness* (lacuna or void, if you like). The Outsider receives a telegram informing him of his mother's death; but he shows no archetypal reaction—no grief, no sense of loss, for example—to that event. The *excess* in him appears when he shoots an Arab. The first bullet killed the Arab, the remaining four were excessive. Archetypally speaking, one can be driven by panic to shoot one bullet out of a primitive instinctual reaction, but with five bullets, there is an excess. The killing of the Arab helps us to distinguish an archetypally limited situation from one that is not archetypal at all. The cause of the Outsider's undoing is attributed to the Sun – one of the Titanic celestial Gods. This sort of projection of the Outsider's guilt onto something so absurd as the Sun belongs very much to Titanism. With some of my patients, I have had to listen to the most ridiculous projections of guilt, blaming everything except themselves which, for me, comes out of the Titanic nature in man.[17] At the end of the book, during a discussion with a priest, Camus shows masterfully the Outsider's inability to make an image. The priest says that prisoners before death usually see the Divine on the stone wall of their cells, but the Outsider replies that he has tried to see the face of his girlfriend, Maria, and has failed.

A Clockwork Orange, extending the theme of the Titanic implicit in Camus' novels, shows total excess all over the place – beatings, killings, rapes, and so forth. The whole of society is excess, "savage and subject to no laws," as Kerényi says of the Titans. Religion has become an easy mimesis which the young Titan uses for his own profit.[18] All of society's institutions are based on this same Titanic excess. And psychiatry, with its Titanic Promethean technology, its missionary zeal, tries to resolve the Titanic riddle for the benefit of the poor Titan, society, and humanity as a whole. Psychiatry as the savior. Prometheus, a more sophisticated Titan, appears in many guises, but closest to our concern is his appearance as the savior in the guise of a technological psychiatrist trying to save the Titan.[19]

Psyche does not learn from Titanic excess. In this connection, we need to make a clear distinction between the suffering, humiliation, pain, and wounds of Psyche – from which psychological learning, knowledge, and soul-making, or soul-initiation, can come – and the repetitive suffering of the Titans – that daily nauseating boredom of the existential level of life.

Certainly, the Titanic personality is the greatest challenge for the soul. So many of the modern psychotherapies try to resolve the soul's conflicts in terms of adaptation to life and 'making it' – a Titanic psychotherapy. Though for a patient in whom the Titanic element is more than just an ingredient, whose dominant personality is Titanic, perhaps the only possible psychotherapy would be to push him into success, making him 'make it.' But this approach is very far from a consciousness that would weaken and make soul.[20] In addition to the *outer* aspects of what has been called external 'human existence,' Titanism can also manifest itself *inwardly*, when excess is inward and so falls into a pathology. We may see this form of Titanism at work in the story of Endymion and his lunar lover, the Moon Goddess Selene. Hesiod's *Theogony* informs us (Kerényi's version):

> The Titaness Theia bore, to her husband Hyperion, Helios, the sun, Selene, the moon, and Eos, the dawn.[21]

There is not much doubt, then, that the Moon, as Selene, was a Titaness. And it is within the difficult mythological and psychological fields which we have been discussing, that we now come to the story of Selene and her love for the shepherd Endymion.

> It was told that when Selene disappeared behind the mountain-crest of Latmos in Asia Minor, she was visiting her lover Endymion, who slept in a cave in that region. Endymion, who in all portrayals of him is shown as a beautiful youth, a herdsman or

> hunter, received the gift of everlasting sleep – doubtless, in the original story, from the moon-goddess herself, so that she could always find him and kiss him in his cave.[22]

I would like us to stay with this picture of Selene going down into the cave to make love with Endymion whenever she wants, to stay with this image *just as it is*. My interest is to read the image, not to synthesize it or amplify its components – Moon as mother, cave as womb, and so on.[23]

Now, as Kerényi informs us, the name "Endymion means one who 'finds himself *within*,' encompassed by his beloved as if in a common garment."[24] We can now begin to imagine what the name Endymion, "the one who finds himself within," might mean. At the most obvious level, it is common enough to say of someone: "Oh yes, so-and-so is a very nice person, but all his energy seems to be inside of him." Or: "It seems to me, so-and-so has a lot of things inside, but he doesn't seem to be able to come out with them." We have all heard this sort of comment about a friend, for example, or a student. And I am sure we can all remember a time in our own lives when whatever we had was only inside, and how we had to wait for it to become something more as our life unfolded. In addition to the meaning of his name as translated by Kerényi, there is another level at which we can reflect upon Endymion living in a cave with the Moon Selene as his lover. For it would seem that Endymion's love with the Moon – who, though a Titaness, is nevertheless a Virgin – keeps him untouched by any other God or Goddess: that is, by other possibilities of life. He remains loyal to his love with the Moon as Selene. We could say that Endymion is a forerunner of Hippolytus, another mythological figure who loved only the Moon – in his case, the Moon as Artemis, a well-defined and consistent image. Endymion is encompassed by his beloved as if by a common garment, which is perhaps to say that he is one who keeps himself virginal. In any case, I think we can connect this inner excess, which we have seen with the story of Endymion and the Titaness Selene, with a peculiar kind of virginity and with a pathology, in contrast with the Titans whose excess appears as outer.

The imagination of the poet Lycophron was stimulated to create a variation of the love-story of Endymion. In Lycophron's account, according to Kerényi, "the god Hypnos, the winged god of sleep, fell in love with Endymion. He gave the youth the ability to sleep with open eyes."[25] This account greatly enriches the complexities of Endymion. We have all, I believe, in certain moments – far more frequently than we are aware – slept through life with open eyes; it is a peculiar lunar state of inner excess. And we can all remember that long period of our youth when we slept with open eyes, endlessly 'mooning around,' to the despair of ourselves and others. Even now, when we want to listen most attentively to an interesting lecture, for example, the God of sleep appears to us and makes us sleep a little bit. I myself can still do a little sleeping with open eyes, sometimes during the most interesting moments of my practice! Then again, it sometimes happens that the reality we have before us, a situation which really hits us, can be so overwhelming that we simply go to sleep with open eyes in front of that event. We retreat within.

Kerényi relates that according to another poet, Apollonius, Endymion's eternal sleep was "a gift from Zeus, who had permitted him to choose his own manner of death: with the result that Endymion had chosen perpetual sleep instead of death."[26] At this point, we can begin to appreciate how these three accounts of Endymion's story cited by Kerényi can give us some insights into the psychological levels I have been hinting at. In the complexities surrounding Endymion, we find, besides the Moon, the figures of Hypnos, Zeus, and death. Of the three accounts, perhaps Apollonius' is the richest and propitiates a deeper psychological view, for Apollonius describes in Endymion a serious pathological condition. In Apollonius' version we have a more profound element; Zeus, the eternal father, intervenes, and the appearance of death turns Endymion's story into a 'serious business.' It is as if Apollonius' imagination shows us Zeus playing *fatefully* with a mortal, as the Gods like to do. Zeus grants Endymion the right to choose the manner of his own death. The theme of choosing one's own manner of death has haunted some poets – especially those Romantic, unbounded poets. To think of choosing one's own way of dying could be seen as having a Titanic, Romantic inflation, coupled with an avoidance of the constant reflection which death plays alongside life – the value of life that comes from the reflection of death. Here we directly confront Endymion's pathology, for we can begin to imagine the Endymion mythologem in terms of a serious illness. By having Endymion choose perpetual sleep instead of death, Apollonius is diagnosing, so to say, the condition of one who has turned the 'death reflection' into a peculiar madness – a condition similar to the one which the German psychiatrist Karl Kahlbaum observed and diagnosed much later in the nineteenth century. In 1874, Kahlbaum coined the word *catatonia* to describe

> that condition in which the patient sits quietly or completely mute and motionless, immovable, with a staring countenance, the eyes fixed on a distant point and apparently completely without volition, without any reaction to sensory impressions, sometimes with a full fledged cerea flexibilitas as in catalepsy.[27]

Can one not view this description of a schizophrenic symptom as the picture of Endymion, lying in a cave, sleeping his perpetual sleep with open eyes, and waiting for the kisses of the Moon, the Titaness Selene?

This state of being, which Kahlbaum described by means of the empirical method (by merit) has already been described by the classical poets, the mythographers of antiquity, with the same precision needed for psychiatric diagnosis, using the beauty of poetry compiled into images – an education of the soul. I cannot imagine that poets like Lycophron or Apollonius had not to some extent experienced in their own bodies something of this lunatic state, conceiving it as the love of the young shepherd Endymion, with the Moon, the Titaness Selene. Indeed, all this sleeping in the cave with Selene, this 'mooning around,' is probably part of poetical activity. These poets of antiquity could be said to have had a corporeal lunatic insight. They were able to find themselves within. And it is just the recovery of this corporeal, or psycho-physical aspect that has been the aim of this paper.

In twentieth-century poetry – and I shall not be referring to poetical re-creations of Endymion – Endymion has appeared in a quite different way: namely, in the *attitudes, explorations*, and the *poetical retinas* of some contemporary poets. André Breton, the great pontiff of Surrealism, wrote in 1928:

> Now I recall Robert Desnos in that epoch that those of us who knew it called *the epoch of dreams*. He "sleeps" but writes and talks. It is night and we are in the studio of my house above the Cabaret Heaven. Outside someone shouts, "Come on, let's go to the Black Cat!" And Desnos goes on seeing what I do not see, what I can only see to the extent he shows it to me.[28]

As is well known, the Surrealists, flourishing in that period *l'entre deux guerres*, were keenly interested in the subconscious. They read a bit of Freud, a bit of alchemy, and a bit about magic. They were steeped in literature. But above all, they were much attracted to Janet's "Psychic Automatism." In the first of the Surrealists' many Manifestos, Breton equated Surrealism with Psychic Automatism. He defined Surrealism as "pure psychic automatism by which it is proposed to express, either verbally, or in any other manner, the real functioning of thought," or "the dictation of thought in the absence of any control exercised by reason, beyond aesthetic or moral preoccupations."[29] Some of them developed an automatic writing technique out of Janet's discovery. They believed they were writing very profound poems by picking up deep messages from the subconscious. I wonder, though, whether these Surrealists knew that at that time, not so very far from Paris, people were working on the theory of the complexes, one of psychology's deepest and most far-reaching theories: how the complexes – those pieces of history – function in us, sometimes automatically. At least, we can say that Janet's discovery was a forerunner of the more serious theory of the complexes.

In addition to their approach to poetry through automatic writing, the Surrealists also wrote a lot about the "Chance Encounter." Lautréamont's phrase, "as beautiful as the chance meeting upon a dissecting table of a sewing machine and an umbrella,"[30] became one of the pillars of Surrealism. At the same time, however, as they deepened their fascination with the "Chance Encounter," there were other people, again, not so very far from Paris, who under the guidance of Richard Wilhelm were studying the theory of synchronicity which he had brought back from China.

Now let us return to Breton's recollection of an evening with Desnos. The scene is captured in a photograph of Desnos lying on a couch in a room above Montparnasse, telling Breton what he is seeing, and creating poetry. I cannot resist connecting him with the image of Endymion, lying sprawled in the beams of the Moon. One can almost see Desnos slipping psycho-physically into the mythologem of Endymion, in love with the Moon – and obviously with poetry, too. Desnos, whom Breton called "the one among us, who is nearest to the Surrealist truth,"[31] *free-associating*, poetically, out of the most autonomous parts of his complexes, keeping himself virginal – encompassed with his beloved as if in a common garment – and untouched by other complexes, except, of course, this virginal one. At that very moment, somebody in the street below shouts, "Let's go to the Black Cat!" And Breton integrates that shout into his meeting with Desnos as a "Chance Encounter," or, if you prefer, a synchronistic event.

Antonio Machado, a great Spanish poet, died in France just a month-and-a-half after the end of the Spanish Civil War, and only two days after the death of his mother. The last image we have of him during his life is of him sitting in a car with his mother on his knees as they cross the Spanish border into France. According to a friend of mine who was one of his disciples, Machado used to walk in a very peculiar way which drew everyone's attention. It seems as if he had some problem with the movement of his body, since he walked in a way that could be described (following Kahlbaum) as catatonic. His living experience of the catatonic was evident in his shuffling steps.

In his book, *Juan de Mairena*, Machado introduced "*el paleto perfecto*." One of those Castilian peasants, with weathered, wrinkled face, wearing a black beret, simple shirt, waistcoat, corduroy trousers, and *alpargatas* (fibre sandals) – that is a paleto. You can still see the paletos in the old Castilian villages of Spain, how they can spend hours sitting on a bench, their eyes staring into nowhere. Machado, with extraordinary grace and humor, gives us his image of the *paleto*:

> *El paleto perfecto es el que nunca se asombra:*
> *ni aun de su propia estupidez.*
>
> [The perfect rustic is he who is never amazed:
> not even at his own stupidity.][32]

With Machado's juxtaposition of the words *perfecto* and *paleto*, we can hear a faint echo of the Castilian mystical ascesis, the way of perfection. Is Machado hinting that the *via* of this ascesis, this perfection, is through the body, that its goal is our *religare* to those parts in us that have to do with the inert body? Is he pointing to another sort of *via regia*? If this is so, then he is on the same track as Jung who says, in his interpretation of the Kundalini Yoga, that its movement for Western man is *down* through the body.[33]

If one of the tasks of poetry is to reflect from death, one can imagine that, for Machado, it was important to explore images which, as we have seen with Endymion, have a peculiar connection with death. Machado's image of *el paleto perfecto* — never astonished, just sitting there, gazing somewhere, not even being aware of being a paleto — is a sort of guarantee that one can have insight, poetically, into the part of us which refuses the reflection of death — the Titanic part which chooses, instead, to sleep perpetually with open eyes.

Remember that the Titan Prometheus did not want to reflect from death; he wanted to liberate men from thinking about death: "I caused men no longer to foresee their death," he proclaims in Aeschylus' drama; "I planted firmly in their hearts blind hopefulness."[34] If we have brought together Machado's *el paleto perfecto* and the mythological figure of Endymion, then we are treading on firm soil, since Machado was the poet for whom death was constantly present throughout his poetry. He belonged to the tradition of poets who have taught that difficult subject — death. Concerning death as a 'serious business,' he writes:

> *Un golpe de ataud en tierra es algo perfectamente serio.*
>
> [A knock (or rap) of the coffin in the earth is something perfectly serious.][35]

Lastly, a final excerpt from still another poet. Listen how the Endymion complex appeared to him at a random moment in the cave of a modern city, in today's common man:

> Or as, when an underground train, in the tube, stops too long
> between stations
> And the conversation rises and slowly fades into silence
> And you see behind every face the mental emptiness deepen
> Leaving only the growing terror of nothing to think about.[36]

1. Helen H. Law, *Bibliography of Greek Myth in English Poetry*, Bulletin XXVII (Oxford, Ohio: American Classical League, 1955), p. 15. Under *Endymion*, forty-two poets are listed.

2. Martin P. Nilsson, *History of Greek Religion*, trans. F.J. Fielden (New York: W.W. Norton, 1964), pp. 143-44.

3. To educate the soul is the concern of many Jungian analysts of the present generation. Soul-making is one of the main themes of the writings of James Hillman. See especially, *Re-Visioning Psychology* (New York: Harper Colophon Books, 1977); also Robert Sardello's excellent paper, *Educating with Soul*, published by The Center for Civic Leadership, The University of Dallas, Irving, Texas.

4. Taken from Martin Heidegger, *Hölderlin y la Esencia de la Poesía*, trans. Juan D. García Bacca (Merida: Universidad de los Andes, 1968), p. 15.
5. Carl Kerényi, *The Gods of the Greeks*, trans. Norman Cameron (London: Thames and Hudson, 1976), p. 20.
6. See Kerényi, *Prometheus: Archetypal Image of Human Existence*, trans. Ralph Mannheim (London: Thames and Hudson, 1963).
7. For me, the archetypes and human existence are the two fields for study. My interest is to enlarge a bit the beachhead which pioneers such as Kerényi have established.
8. Marie-Louise von Franz already saw something similar in her discussion of the Puer in connection with Bruno Goetz's *Reich Ohne Raum*. However, where she saw only the Puer, I am suggesting also the presence of a Titanic element.
9. José Lezama Lima, "Las Imágenes Posibles" in *Esferaimagen* (Barcelona: Tusquets Editor, 1970), p. 51ff.
10. Nilsson, p. 144.
11. *Ibid*., p. 23.
12. If we were to follow Kerényi on this point and agree that the Titans represent a particular function, then the Titans, with their excessiveness, could be called the archetype of excess.
13. In discussing modern manifestations of the Titanic, I would like to stay within the containers of *The Outsider* and *A Clockwork Orange* (which I presume most everyone has read).
14. See note 11.
15. We have to realize that there are two kinds of rhetoric: the archetypal and the Titanic. The Titanic rhetoric can be detected in references such as, "That is mere rhetoric."
16. E.R. Dodds, *The Greeks and the Irrational* (Berkeley: University of California Press, 1968), p. 156.
17. I would like to draw attention to this connection between guilt and Titanism as seen from the perspective of Archetypal Psychology. It could be useful. Both the projection of guilt and the carrying of all the guilt upon oneself are Titanic. It is to be noted that, generally speaking, psychotherapy tries to cure the projection by getting the patient to take in the guilt he so loosely and Titanically projects, and in the second case, by encouraging the patient to blame the parents, society, or whatever. Both are Titanic "solutions" which have nothing to do with a psychotherapy that moves the soul through images.
18. One has only to think of religious cults, like the one led by Jim Jones, or of the Titan Menoetius – whose name means "he whom mortal doom awaits" – to get a sense of the religious zeal which dwells in the Titanic.
19. I should perhaps mention here that this Titanic excess is not only the concern of psychopathology. Titanic excess has also to do with the medical term *stress*, but this medical interest in the Titanic takes us beyond our purposes.
20. Recently I have heard of the very Titanic conception of trying to "cure" psychosis (a broken archetype) by pushing the patient into psychopathy, pushing the patient into the mimetic Titanic world.
21. Kerényi, *The Gods of the Greeks*, p. 22.
22. *Ibid*., p. 198.
23. It is clear from Kerényi's account that Selene reserves the right to make the first move towards Endymion; the shepherd is depicted as reclining passively and awaiting her amorous advance. Walter Otto adds that it is characteristic of Titanesses to make the first move in an erotic encounter.

24. Kerényi, *The Gods of the Greeks*, p. 198.

25. *Ibid.*

26. *Ibid.*

27. Lawrence C. Kolb, *Modern Clinical Psychiatry*, eighth edition (London: W.B. Saunders Co., 1973), p. 309.

28. André Breton, *Nadja* (Mexico: Edition Joaquin Mortiz, 1963), p. 22. This and later passages in English are my own translations from the Spanish.

29. Breton, "Primer Manifiesto," in *Manifiestos del Surrealismo* (Madrid: Ediciones Guadarrama, S.A., 1974), p. 44.

30. J.H. Matthews, *An Introduction to Surrealism* (University Park, Pennsylvania: The Pennsylvania State University Press, 1965), p. 105.

31. Breton, "Primer Manifiesto," *Manifiestos del Surrealismo*, p. 48.

32. Antonio Machado, in *Obras Completas* (Madrid: Editorial Plenitud), "Juan de Mairena," p. 1153. For English translation see Ben Belitt (Berkeley: University of California Press, 1963).

33. Jung, in his seminar on the Interpretation of the Kundalini Yoga, makes it clear that the Kundalini Yoga can be useful for Westerners if the movement is downward, a reverse of the upward movement conceived for the Eastern mind. Western man starts out up in Vishuda (the throat region, the logos), and so is in need of coming down into those regions of the body alien to him. Jung's insights have to do with the repression of the body in Western Christian culture. My psychotherapeutical conception very much takes into account Jung's vision of this downward movement into the body, the importance of activating the historically repressed body, as well as activating the archetypes of the body —how one imagines one's own body. Jung's interpretation for the Westerner gives a useful background for diagnosing the Westerner's superficial mimetic literal approach to the Kundalini Yoga. Machado, with his poetical image, calls our attention to the body which Western man finds so difficult to animate. See *Spring 1975*, "Psychological Commentary on Kundalini Yoga," Lectures One and Two—1932, p. 1; and *Spring 1976*, Lectures Three and Four—1932, p. 1 (Zürich: Spring Publications).

34. Aeschylus, *Prometheus Bound*, trans. Philip Vellacott (Harmondsworth: Penguin Classics, 1961), p. 28.

35. Machado, "En el Entierro de un Amigo," *Obras Completas*, p. 852.

36. T.S. Eliot, "East Coker," III, *Four Quartets,* in *The Complete Poems and Plays* (London: Faber and Faber, 1969), p. 180.

Virginities of Image

Patricia Berry-Hillman

Since offering the title for this lecture, I have been trying to remember what I meant by it. Whatever my initial intuition, it could not have been an obvious one, for what we mean in imaginal psychology by image is by no means virginal; an image is never pure, never virginal. Even the 'idea' of image is unclear. Sometimes we speak of image as though it were a thing, and sometimes we mean by it a way of seeing or hearing.

Image is a complexity of relationships, an inherence of tensions, juxtapositions, and interconnections. An image is neither pure meaning, nor pure relations, nor pure perception. It is not even pure reflection, for one can never say with certainty that this is 'the thing' and that a reflection of the thing. Nor can one say that image is *this* literally and *that* metaphorically. These dualities – thing *versus* reflection, literal *versus* metaphorical – are not images but rather ways of structuring images.

The imaginal is never virginally pure but always ambiguous, shady, and slightly disreputable, a mixture of shade and light, contour and shadow. With image, modalities intrude. Meanings interpenetrate. Fantasy and perception break into each other; idea and fact transgress each other's borders. The virginal resists these intrusions, these interpenetrations, these impurities. In this sense, we can say the virgin is that which resists the imagistic. And this is my first main theme: *to resist the image is to be virginal in psyche, and to be a psychic virgin is to be closed to the image*.

Resistance is necessary for the virginal integrity of the body of the image. Image *is* a body—a psychic body that holds tension and supports being. Though we foolishly interpret, simplistically allegorize, reduce meanings to symbols and signs, nevertheless the image remains—never changing, never yielding. Like the inscrutable, virginal sphinx,[1] the image puzzles us with questions but yields no answers.

Resistance has different forms, and the virginal can resist in many ways. Resistance may take the form of the virgin Hippolytus, for whom virginity means *exclusivity* — the exclusive worship of one divinity. Hippolytus is dedicated solely to the chaste, free spirit of Artemis. He rejects the Aphroditic which would entangle him in the complications of sensuality and erotic involvement. Hippolytus is interested in distant beauty—not sensuality, an intercourse which would allow the image to move in and through him. He enjoys hunting the image (tracking it down) but not its embrace. Hippolytus does not realize he is in image, but sees image as something remote to be pursued. His far-ranging spirit remains unfettered and chaste, pure and keen-sighted in the distant, free realm of the woods. Artemisian spirit is indeed part of image: free as its spontaneity, its hidden life, its appeal to our curiosity. But the exclusive worship of this freedom, distance, and curiosity is doomed to fail; in the myth of Hippolytus, doomed to fail tragically.

Now, what can we make of this pattern in terms of image? We are familiar with images that present this free, soaring, Artemisian sense: images seemingly unconnected with civilization and society, the close-at-hand, the near — those small, involving details, the entanglements of daily life we experience with family, spouse, children, acquaintances. For a votary of Artemis, image embodies none of these entanglements. Hippolytus is inviolate, appreciative, and reverent, but at the same time untouched, not embodied by the body of image.

When fascinated by this ephemeral, Artemisian aspect of image, sight becomes far-sighted; implications become far-reaching like Artemis' arrows. Feelings soar impersonally beyond the here-and-now, above the tangles of the immediate, the mess of the petty, personal details of everyday life. Here is an account by an American woman in Europe of a dream that captures something of this feeling.

> I was standing in line at the Zentral Bibliothek to get a book. I realized that the language everyone was speaking was a dialect I didn't understand. I panicked, wondering how I was going to ask for the books I needed. A tall woman came up to me and, putting her arm around me, took me past the line and up to the window to get the books. We then walked together through the streets. It was night. I felt elated that I'd been able to finish my research. Tremendous freedom. We walked what seemed like all night, as though through an amusement park. Lights flashed, things twirled and flickered in the distance like rides (roller coasters, Ferris wheels, etc.). Then she took me into a harshly-lit cafeteria. The place was ugly and the people shabby. Suddenly she put her arm around me and put her hand into my pants. I was horrified and pushed her away violently.

The tone of the first part of this dream is Artemisian. A tall woman figure guides the dreamer to the books she desires. The dreamer feels inspired and free; her spirit soars. Amusement lights flash and flicker – in the distance, notice, not the nearness. Then the whole scene turns, and in the not-so-clean well-lighted place (where food is served in harsh light), the woman who hitherto had been a spirited Artemisian guide now turns, in a most un-Artemisian way, grossly physical. The virginally pure aspect of the image seems to have turned upon itself and shifted downward, focusing inappropriately below the belt. The image has plunged from its high-flying, inspirational virginity, shocking the dreamer into an awareness that her body is also part of the situation. The body, the sexual, forms part of the image—finding the book is also being found in the body and being harshly violated.

Interpreting this dream, one can easily be caught by its virginal spirit and thus side exclusively (purely, virginally) with one aspect of the dream – depending upon the penchant of the analyst, with either the 'upward,' non-physical or the 'downward,' physical, grosser aspect. But an image includes all of its aspects, as the dream shows. The woman figure who inspires the spirit at the same time lowers the dreamer into her lower nature through the impurity of sexuality.

The virginal may appear in another pattern of image work. The virgin Narcissus reflects endlessly, purely upon himself. As the clear pool of this reflection ripples in death, Narcissus raptures ever deeper. The movement is profound. Narcissistic reflection is deeply self-revealing and self-contained, alchemically enclosed within the narrow limits of the pond. But despite this depth of vertical reflection, or perhaps because of it, the horizontal world of Echo is ignored. In the tale, Echo pines away, longing for the narcissistic reflection that excludes her. Let us say that Echo is the echoing of what is 'out-there' – objects, the daily, others, the lateral. Narcissus ignores these reverberations from surfaces, things around. Attempting to find insight and meaning within oneself, one becomes deaf to surroundings.

Image work seems to invite this narcissistic virginity. Because reflection and depth are so vitally important, image tends to draw one into 'vertical' rather than 'horizontal' reflection. But the Lopez maxim, "stick to the image," does not necessitate a mesmerized downward stare. Depth can also mean a depth within, a penetration of the immediate, across and through surfaces.

Although narcissistic virginity denies the horizontal, Narcissus unlike other virgins does not flee from the physical; rather, he flees into it. It is the less physical realm of sounds and echoes that he fears. As sound, Echo cannot be touched, cannot be concretized. The essence of Echo is precisely in the reverberations, the hiatus, the space between. Whereas the image can remain virginal if it is held – narcissistically – too close, Echo requires distance, breadth.

Dreams in which one is rejected, betrayed, made jealous, failed, create the distance needed for echo to sound. In these dreams, emptiness is created, room established, attachments dissolved, sensuality irrelevant. The movement is one of echoing out of oneself, beyond physical attachments, and attachments to the physical, into a broader, more substantial, wider-ranging world.

The virgin Cassandra offers us another pattern of the virginal. Whereas Hippolytus denies Aphrodite consciousness and Narcissus, Echo – Cassandra resists the Apollonic. Apollo, in his passion for Cassandra, bestows on her the gift of prophecy. But when Cassandra refuses him, preferring to remain virginally untouched, Apollo swears that none shall believe her prophecies. Cassandra's virginity denies Apollonic consciousness, denies the formality and clarity of image work, denies that ideas can be abstracted from images, connections made, thoughts formed, things structured.

Sometimes dreams speak quite directly about the necessity of form. For example, an analysand having difficulty writing a paper dreamt that she was sitting in her office writing when suddenly she heard crying. Huddled in the corner was a black woman, who, sobbing, held up a string of African beads.

It would seem that the sobbing woman made a direct appeal concerning form. The manner in which the analysand was writing evidently hurt the black woman, who offered another mode more loosely connected, like beads on a string. Structure need not be logically deductive but might be, as in this case, circular and still be formally exact.

In general one might say that images contain particular forms, that there is a formal element within the image. But Cassandra virginity denies this formality so that attempts to bring out the structure of a thought or image seem a violation: a dream too precious to be written down, feelings too deep to be spoken, intuitions too subtle to be articulated. When one is in this virginal mood, Apollonic clarity and exactitude feel threatening, "just academic" or "only a head trip." Cassandra needs to be misunderstood. Her perceptions and intuitions do not lack insight. In truth they are quite acute, but they lack effect, the power of persuasion, or *peitho*.

Peitho is important. In Aeschylus' *Agamemnon* it is not that Cassandra's words go unheard – the chorus hears what she is saying – but her words have no *effect*; her prophecies do not touch the principal characters or influence the course of action. This inability to influence, to formulate effectively, is Cassandra's purity.

Of course we all have something of this virginity – particularly when we turn prophetic. Thoughts that have no effect in the here-and-now get projected into the future. When 'what-is' lacks persuasiveness, it becomes 'what *will be*,' in the guise of literal foretelling or warning.

In analysis we tend to make these prophetic or prognostic declamations when we cannot articulate the material. When an image in a dream fails to convey a sense of psychic reality, or when our feelings for the dream lack *peitho*, we tend to project this lack as a power into the future. Cassandra virginity, by running from formal articulation, loses touch with the persuasive power of the image.

We have mentioned now three mythic patterns of virginity: Hippolytus, Narcissus, and Cassandra. All have in common an absence of body in relation to image – whether that absence is of the physical body (as in the case of Hippolytus), or the body as world (Narcissus), or the body of form and persuasion (Cassandra). In each instance, the body aspect of image remains untouched so that the virginity of psyche is untouched by the image.

In addition to these mythic styles of virginity, let us turn to some aesthetic styles; for these I call upon poetry, an art which has long dealt with the subtleties and problems of image. But poetry, too, has a virginal aspect. As Robert Penn Warren observes in his essay "Pure and Impure Poetry,"[2] if a poem were entirely pure (in our terms, virginal), it would no longer be a poem; a good or complete poem requires impurity.

Warren's idea holds not only for the poetics of poetry but also for the poetics of psyche; that is, for the poetics of dreams. Of course, there are differences between poems and dreams, but let us look at their poetic similarities. Consider Shelley's "The Cloud":

> I bring fresh showers for the thirsting flowers,
> From the seas and the streams;
> I bear light shade for the leaves when laid
> In their noonday dreams.
> From my wings are shaken the dews that waken
> The sweet buds every one,
> When rocked to rest on their mother's breast,
> As she dances about the sun.

Now in terms of image these are fairly insubstantial lines. They lack irony or, in psychological terms, have little self-awareness or reflective consciousness. Poetically they acquire some tension through form and rhyme scheme. But this tension is not particularly fertile. The "I" who is the cloud simply carries on powerfully, descriptively, with little trouble or complication.

Now let me read you part of a dream that seems comparable. The dreamer is a woman in her 30's.

> I came to a building site and had difficulty going on because there was a big bulldozer with iron, blade-like teeth. The driver did not see me for it kept coming very near. Then I began dancing. As I danced I felt great power and magic and the machine was driven away.

The dream tells of a dancing ego personality, the "I" in the dream, so powerful in her charm that she dances away the bulldozer — a building machine that would clear the ground and prepare the virginal earth for construction. The power of the dreamer's magic dance keeps all this potential work of the bulldozer at bay. The dream reveals an effective defense.

As you might imagine, the dreamer was a *femme fatale* – magical, mediumistic, and powerful – who had literally seduced her way through life's difficulties. Her dance knew no limits. Whatever threatened her, she slept with. But this magical dance had also kept her virginal, effectively blocking the process of construction, any encroachment of civilization or culture.

Both dream and poem have a kind of tension – the poem in its form and the dream in its content: dancer threatened by bulldozer. But both dream and poem remain virginal images because they lack a crucial kind of tension, what Susanne Langer would call "fecundity."[3] A fecund tension breaks through the surface of what is happening and creates a surprising, difficult, or unaccustomed moment. So, the virginity of an image is not deflowered by just any kind of tension, but only by a fecund tension, a tension that does something, turns the earth or surprises the cloud, breaks through the accustomed. If an image is not to remain virginal, it needs this fecund tension.

Let us turn now to another mode of the aesthetic virginal: the virginal as self-same or self-enclosed. As an example of this virginity, note a poem by Landor entitled "Dying Speech of an Old Philosopher."

> I strove with none, for none was worth my strife:
> Nature I loved, and next to Nature, Art:
> I warmed both hands before the fire of Life;
> It sinks; and I am ready to depart.

The poem is self-enclosed, so that even as death approaches we find nothing abrupt or jagged, nothing cacophonous. The poem remains at one with its feeling, unruffled, and relatively uninteresting. As a virginal image, the poem is an idealized mood. Compare this with another of Landor's poems on the theme of death. This poem too begins virginally.

> Mild is the parting year, and sweet
> The odor of the falling spray;
> Life passes on more rudely fleet,
> And balmless is its closing day.[4]

This poem, in contrast to the first, begins to show complexity in its juxtaposition of "rudely fleet" and "balmless." It goes on to describe the close of life:

> I wait its [life's] close, I court its gloom,
> But mourn that never must there fall
> Or on my breast or on my tomb
> The tear that would have soothed it all.

The poem's initial virginity is effectively broken by the last stanza. Progressively the simple perception of the first lines is interpenetrated by more complex emotions. In the second stanza the "I" waits its close, courts its gloom, and mourns. Waiting, courting, and mourning are three quite distinct emotions, any of which alone might be merely virginal. In succession, however, the movement becomes increasingly complex as each feeling breaks apart or opens the previous.

This non-virginal complexity is certainly a psychological achievement. It is not ambivalence; the poem is quite firm in its direction. Nor is it complexity for the sake of complexity. At this point, it would be easy to say that complexity in itself is the non-virginal and therefore our aim. But there are all sorts of complexity, including the simply associative or decorative. The virgin bedecked with jewels and robes, halos, embroidery, and glitter may *appear* 'complex,' but she is not necessarily transformative. An ornate baroque image is not necessarily more interesting than, say, a simple, classic one, on the sole ground that the one image is complex and the other is not. Similarly, psychological associations, esoteric amplifications, and symbols do not by themselves transform virginity but may merely adorn and cover it further. We must not confuse the fecundity of an image with complications that have been added to it.

Indeed, the non-virginal may be quite simple — as imagistic poetry or haiku is simple. The simple may also be the essential. Williams' "red wheelbarrow glazed with rain"[5] is terse, but this terseness crystallizes. The refined condensations that we find in imagistic poetry and in the most beautiful calligraphy are achievements of essence, highly refined moments. The simple is not always the simplistic or subjective, as critics of imagism maintain.[6]

As virginal, the image holds something 'more-than' the simple or innocent; it contains something divine. Not only the Virgin

Mary, but also most pagan goddesses carry the epithet *parthenos*, or "virgin."[7] Athena, Artemis, Persephone, Hestia—but also Hera and Aphrodite—are called *Parthenos*. Hera the wife and Aphrodite the lover have virginal qualities. As these divine figures psychologically encompass more than mere biology, so too does virginity refer to a psychic state.

For the Greeks, any child born of an unmarried mother was considered virginal.[8] The epithet *parthenos* applied to the children of concubines or prostitutes—indeed any child whose 'father' was not the man in the living room. In other words, the father of the virgin is the absent, the unknown, or the spirit 'father.'[9]

The father of a virgin image cannot be known. Our petty inquiries into the 'history' of a poem, our researches into influences or the author's biography, our attempts to determine cultural causes and personal traumas, to detail the "affective needs" that a poem satisfies – all miss the point.[10] And psychology, which should perhaps know most about this virgin state of the psyche, is often most ignorant, insensitive, positivistic, and causalistic about it.

When working with dreams, we sometimes disparage a simple scene or statement by calling it a dream fragment. These 'fragments' often embarrass the dreamer, as though there *should* be more, as though our psyches should be interestingly complex and engaged with fascinating symbols. These analytical judgments are comparable, in literary terms, to the judgment of one genre in terms of another—to the view of an imagistic poem, say, from the perspective of a rambling Dostoyevsky narrative; or, in our terms, to the view of the dream, a product of Hades, from the perspective of a tumbling, ever-fluid life.

Imagism in dreams may show as depressive. In such moments, the psyche appears tightened, coagulated, stuck without movement. Psychic imagism can thus be the poetic cure for too much life by returning us to what is tight, essential, and bone-like. Dreams of death, dying, deserts, of consuming or being consumed, blocked, imprisoned, constrained, stopped, parched, express the importance of this poetic process. Here again the simple, imagistically sparse is by no means the virginal.

In fact the virginal may appear as quite the contrary. Virginity can be fluid, flirtatious, loquacious, bubbly and pointless; it can be fiery, quick and fantastic. There are dreams in which so much seems to happen and yet little does, despite the apparently transformative imagery, as in the following: "a hawk with a mickey mouse mask dove at me...it turned into flames that then turned blue and green and then with clutching, hand-like movements climbed up a telephone pole."

Fantastical dreams seem to be working to turn natural perception into more complicated perception by means of the unnatural or surrealistic. It is as though perception is working on itself in an attempt to make a psychological difference. But insofar as this difference is *only* fantastical, the psyche is still virginal, as though fascinated with its own frivolousness.

The following lines show the fantastical combined with subjectivism:

> I am the cause, I am a stockpile of chemical
> toys, my body
> is a deadly gadget,
> I reach out in love, my hands are guns,
> my good intentions are completely lethal.[11]

Here the lethal has been exaggerated to the fantastic and then infused with subjectivity. The poet has identified with the lethal as though the world of warfare were one with subjective feeling.

Eliot's warning concerning the personal is important here. "Poetry is not a turning loose of emotion, but an escape from emotion; it is not the expression of personality, but an escape from personality."[12] The poem must be depersonalized, or at least more distant and complex than personal, subjective feelings.

The virginal, as we have seen, is a fantastic, personal, or simplistic quality of mind. Aesthetically as well as psychologically, the virginal is an innocence, a naiveté to be penetrated psychologically and worked artistically. But we have also implied that the virginal is part of the image. I would now add that *the virgin is not only part of, but even crucial to the image*. We have imagined the virginal as resistance, an aspect of the psyche that wishes not to yield. But while resisting intrusion, the virgin also gives it form; that is, the purity in the image gives the image form. The way in which a poem is pure — fantastically, simplistically, or subjectively — requires particular artistic moves, particular kinds of impurity for the poem to cohere.

For an application of these moves to dreams, we can recall the example of the dancer and the bulldozer. At the narrative level, we might say that the dancer drove the bulldozer away. Imagistically (or from the point of view of image), however, we can also say that the dancer is the occasion of the machine's coming; both occur together. The seductress and the bulldozer each form part of the building site. The dancer is also a condition *for* construction.

A fecund tension is required. The psyche needs tension to create the intensity with which to work. And the purity of the virgin's resistance is crucial to this intensity.

The virgin is 'uptight' because the virgin indeed has something to protect: a dedication to the impersonal and its values. As the virginal aspect in a poem protects the poem, so in a dream it protects the dream. The icon of the virgin on the wall, the image of the Virgin as symbol, is testament to the eternal virginity of image, its pure and inviolate nature. The virgin depicts not only the image of virginity, but the virginity of image intact unto itself.

The virgin of unknown father, as virgin mother, is self-generative. This parthenogenesis is the generativity of the imagination. Yet — and I would not want to end without some final conundrum — the virgin is virginal only insofar as there is something which is also non-virginal: the *beata culpa*. Imagistically, purity and impurity go hand-in-hand. It is the impurity of an image or a poem that protects its purity. Eliot's *Waste Land* ends with *Shantih, shantih, shantih* — a feeling of pure but hard-earned peace. These final lines of *Shantih* ring with such beauty, integrity — and virginity — because of the extraordinary impurity of the poem that has preceded; the "heap of broken images," the "wrinkled dugs," the rat "dragging its slimy belly on the bank" — a teeming richness of complex, sophisticated impurity that readies us for a peace of integrity. This is not the simplistic peace of a virgin — naive, innocent, unspoilt — but the peace of an imaginal achievement. Alchemically, this is not the virgin as *prima materia* (the milky unconscious), but the virgin as a recovery of something worked.

William Butler Yeats, at the age of seventy-two. wrote in one of his last poems:

> Those masterful images because complete
> Grew in pure mind, but out of what began?
> A mound of refuse or the sweepings of a street,
> Old kettles, old bottles, and a broken can,
> Old iron, old bones, old rags, that raving slut
> Who keeps the till. Now that my ladder's gone,
> I must lie down where all the ladders start,
> In the foul rag-and-bone shop of the heart.[13]

The pure of which Yeats speaks would seem the virginal achievement of image. The mound of refuse, the raving slut, the foul rag-and-bone shop of the heart are the impurities that give integrity to the virginity of the image.

1. The sphinx was called *parthenos*, "virgin." See W.H. Roscher, *Lexikon der Griechischen und Römischen Mythologie*, VII (Hildesheim: Olms, 1965), pp. 153-4.
2. Robert Penn Warren, "Pure and Impure Poetry," *Critical Theory Since Plato*, ed. Hazard Adams (New York: Harcourt Brace Jovanovich, 1971), pp. 981-992.
3. Susanne Langer speaks of the "principle of fecundity," by which she means that an idea must be not only true but interesting. Cf. Susanne Langer, *Feeling and Form* (New York: Scribner's, 1953), p. 8.
4. Walter Savage Landor, "Mild Is the Parting Year, and Sweet."
5. William Carlos Williams, "The Red Wheelbarrow."
6. As an example of criticism that confuses the simple with the simplistic, see Philip Wheelwright, *Metaphor and Reality* (Bloomington/London: Indiana University Press, 1968), pp. 159 ff.
7. See Roscher for a list of those divinities bearing the epithet *parthenos*. See also J.M. Robertson, *Christianity and Mythology*, 2nd edition (London: Watts & Co., 1910), p. 293. Robertson's list includes Aphrodite, Hera, Demeter, Cybele, Leto, and Isis.
8. See *parthenios*, Liddell & Scott, *A Greek-English Lexicon*.
9. See John Layard, *The Virgin Archetype* (Zürich: Spring Publications, 1977), particularly pp. 288 ff on the connection between virgin and spirit.
10. In this regard see particularly essays by Hippolyte Taine, Sigmund Freud, and I.A. Richards in *Critical Theory Since Plato*, ed. Hazard Adams.
11. From the Margaret Atwood poem, "It's Dangerous to Read Newspapers."
12. T.S. Eliot, "Tradition and the Individual Talent."
13. From "The Circus Animals' Desertion."

The Landscape of Virginity

Robert J. Sardello

John Layard has written the seminal essay sensitizing us to the archetypal psychology of virginity. Virginity, Layard convincingly shows, is a necessity of the soul. It refers neither to absence of nor abstinence from intercourse but rather to the transformation of a basic instinct for union with the mother into a desire for spiritual union with the soul; virginity is a primary telos of the individual soul.

What I have to add to Layard's genius consists of little more than another look at that psychic topography from the stance of cultural psychology. Cultural psychology is not another psychology; it is a particular way of doing archetypal psychology – a way of emphasizing that soul is not some interior thing, that image is not private. It is an archetypal psychology emphasizing the action of soul in world.

Cultural psychology relies on memory, in the sense described by Robert Duncan – the place where the high and the low intermingle "bewilderingly," memory as the eruptions of the divine in the trivial. This psychology, in the service of Mnemosyne, is concerned with the therapy of individual life in culture. Mnemosyne, Mother of the Muses, brings the gods into active, playful, artful speech, uniting their fateful workings with the world we daily inhabit, making a bond or bridge between the world available to our senses and the ever-present actions of the gods.

The word *transformation* makes the events of psychological life appear to pass more smoothly and with greater ease than they are actually experienced. How simple it is to speak of virginity as 'the transformation from instinctual bond to spiritual union'; how simple to reduce Layard's intricate anthropology. Such a tendency to simplify and reduce what the psyche experiences, to speak conclusively rather than imagistically, to let matters of the soul drift upward into the mind, introduces a more materialistic perspective into psychology. I am not suggesting, however, the introduction of gross materialism but rather the realization that soul belongs to this world, that the matters of the soul can be found happening in the midst of things. The action of virginizing shows forth in the landscape and in the architecture that gathers that landscape together to form a place. I would like to be able to show this directly by doing a psychological reading of some particular place in the contemporary world. However, I must work through the *memory* of a place which clearly shows forth the action of virginity, hoping that the memory will allow us to perceive more imagistically the world we now inhabit. This place is the temple of Demeter at Eleusis.

Contemporary architecture does not lend itself readily to a reading in terms of its archetypal imagery because our present architecture is largely a product of our intellectual and technical concerns. Its primary reference is no longer the gods but man, who is defined by what he can do rather than by who is working through him. Modern functional design concentrates on solving practical problems, particularly those thrown up by the inhuman conditions of our nineteenth-century cities. Functionalism devises a logic of pure functional form which architects such as Le Corbusier have attempted to endow with a sense of beauty. A great freedom flows from emphasis on spatial structure alone, but the price of this freedom is the disappearance of a cultural tradition and of a visible psychic life. The psyche, left without a world, resorts to its own spontaneity, presenting life with essential patterns in the fragmented form of dreams. But the dream fragments lack the sustaining background of a landscape. Psychic topography takes on not only depth but body and substance when placed against the background of the geography and architecture of the temple of Demeter at Eleusis. This substantial, ecological psychology defies the tendency of the mind to look upon the word *transformation* as *conclusion*.

*

The Homeric Hymn to Demeter is a song of the action of virginity in Layard's sense, the transformation of instinctual union to spiritual bond. The Hymn tells of Hades' rape of Demeter's daughter, Persephone, and of Demeter's desperate search and grieving for her daughter. The setting is the Nycaean Plain. Persephone is playing apart from Demeter, gathering flowers in the midst of "deep grassy meadows." As Persephone reaches to pick a narcissus – "a glorious hundred-fold blossom" – the Earth gapes and Hades shoots straight out of a chasm on a glittering chariot pulled by immortal horses; he grabs Persephone and carries her away. Hecate and Helios hear the screams, and Demeter hears the echo of her cries "from the heights of the mountains and the depths of the ocean."

Demeter, seized by anguish, searches for Persephone nine days and nine nights, carrying torches to guide her over the surface of the Earth. On the tenth morning, Demeter meets Hecate and then Helios; neither can help find the daughter, although Helios tells Demeter that Zeus has given Persephone to his brother Hades, who bore her off to the Underworld to be his wife.

Demeter withdraws, wandering aimlessly, and finally comes to the town of Eleusis. She sits, distraught, near a well called the Virgin's Well. The daughters of Celeus come by to draw water from the well. Taking the disguise of an old woman, Demeter tells the maidens a false story of how she came to be there and asks if she may work in their home perhaps taking care of a child. The maidens inform their mother, who instructs them to bring the woman to the house. At first, Demeter sits on a chair grieving without speaking, smiling, eating, or drinking. But Iambe, one of the daughters of Celeus, makes Demeter smile in response to her joking and clowning and obscene gestures; Demeter's grief becomes tenderness.

Demeter takes the son of the house, Demophoon, under her care and the child grows like a god, even though he is given nothing to eat. Each night Demeter lays Demophoon into the fire, like a log. Eventually the child's mother discovers this repeated act and cries out in horror. Demeter turns in anger, reveals herself as Demeter, and states that the mortals do not know whether good or evil approaches. Demeter would have made the boy immortal, but now he is to remain mortal. Demeter demands that a temple be built above the well. Zeus finally sends Hermes to recover Persephone, but Hades allows her to leave only after she has eaten a pomegranate seed to assure her return.

A cultural psychology remembers this hymn as it is enacted in the actions of people serving this image: communal actions forming the culture of the soul. The virginizing action takes place along a sacred path leading from Athens to Eleusis. At the climax of the Eleusinian mysteries—which are an imitation of Demeter's loss and recovery of Persephone — a day-long procession winds its way dancing and singing from Athens through the pass of Daphni onto the Eleusinian Plain; it circles round the shore of the Gulf of Eleusis and finally arrives in the evening at the temple of Demeter. The route follows a repetitive path of "losing and finding," a labyrinthian path. The site of the temple is first hidden from view by a mountain, then suddenly it appears and disappears again. Instinct moves by repetition; the action of transformation is no straight-line affair. The instinctual body is never left behind. Little bits of insight circle around and back to envelop and intertwine with the instinctual body, constantly confusing long-range vision.

Mount Kerata—a name which means "horned"—rises above the sanctuary at Eleusis. This site is a passage between worlds, between the "Gates of Horn." (The word *Eleusis* itself means "passage" or "gate.") One does not pass through the gates directly. The virginizing action begins with the formation of the procession in Athens, the Sacred Labyrinthian Path, and the ritual acts within the temple. The temple itself gathers together the beginning, the passages, the losing of Persephone, the grieving of Demeter, the persistence of coming closer and closer to the Underworld, the encounter with the Underworld, and the mystery of that encounter. The temple repeats what is already being enacted ten miles away, what is experienced in the pilgrimage, and the event itself. At the beginning of the path in Athens, initiates fast in their homes for nine days, an act which makes them more sensitive to the movements of the body and to the ceremonies they will undergo. The path of the journey makes its impression on the sensitized body; the goal of the journey and the journey itself are inseparable—the losing is a finding and the finding is a losing. Anxiety is the mode of this journey of the soul. The site of the temple itself intensifies the experience.

> Directly ahead of the outer propylaia is the grotto of Hades, a natural cave in a rock toward which the procession directly leads. The cavern is partly masked by walls, however, and the proces-

> sion would have been required to swing half left through the smaller propylaia in order to come to the grotto beyond it on the right hand. Having come first to the cave of death, the way passes beyond it and curves snakelike upward to the left around the side of the hill.[1]

The landscape of instinctual transformation, Demeter/Persephone landscape, is completely pervaded by the qualities of "losing and finding," the qualities of "passage," and the qualities of a paradoxical relation between "beginning and ending." The landscape is repetitious, just as every instinctual action – eating, sexual expression, breathing, fear – is repetitious. Repetitious, but not monotonous, as if a signal that something important is happening. We may feel uncertain, however, wondering whether it is not more of the same old thing, like our compulsions, our drives, our impulses. We are never sure whether we are losing something or finding something, or both. Just when we think we have passed through an obsession, there it is again – and if our body is not sensitive to what is happening, we cannot notice that it is just slightly, ever so slightly different. The passage through Demeter/Persephone landscape shows us this topography of instinctual action. The horned mountain of Kerata is a gate; another gate awaits us at the temple site; the natural cave at the temple site is but one of many passages; indeed, the journey itself is a passage, beginning during the day and ending at the gate of the temple, passage from day to night. The relation between beginning and ending is similarly repetitious. The rites begin with nine days of fasting in the home, marking the end of ordinary life. The pilgrimage begins at the river Illisos which ends one sacrifice and begins another passage. The journey ends at the sanctuary which begins the sacred mystery rites.

The qualities of landscape suggest that instinct moves by repetition and that repetition deepens into soul through the daily moments of bodily life. It suggests that instinctual movement is difficult, full of bitterness (see James Hillman's paper), thwarted expectation, imagination obscured (see Patricia Berry's paper), all in the service of making little differences make a difference. Perception is sharpened in this kind of landscape. The senses become acute, made painfully aware that something is happening, without being able to imagine exactly what is going on. Berry indicates this significance of Demeter to our soul:

> [Demeter's] basic, underlying mood is heavily earthy and under-earthy. Not for long is she an enthusiast, nor I believe is she one who searches for 'meaning' and 'truth.' She searches merely for her daughter [i.e., for her virginity] – that underworld component which belongs by birth to her. And with this kinship tie comes her significance, and the significance of everything she does. Whether she cooks with this kind of ingredient or another makes a difference – not because one is designed to dispel the 'unnatural' effects of civilization, but because the taste is different – and that *does* make a difference.... It is not because some lore of meaning is attached to thyme and another to rosemary, but because to Demeter's taste they are *sensually* different. And the sensual, daily moments of life when viewed in terms of underlife (death) become discrete, separate, and each moment of sensation becomes significant. There is no way that life may be experienced as "just life," just getting on, making do. Life takes on a significance of the senses. The senses become so wholly life-giving because sensation reaches to and incorporates the underworld.[2]

This sense of sensing differences is enacted in the psychic landscape of Demeter: the pain of instinct learning to sense differences.

To look again at this movement into virginity, let us pay attention to the architecture of the sanctuary in the Temple to Demeter at Eleusis.

First, we come to the Virgin's well, called the *Kallichoron*, "well of the beautiful dances." The circular well, protected by the outer wall of the sanctuary, is surrounded by stone pavement. Here circle dances are performed. Surely, the form of the dance is a circular movement to the left, counter to Demeter's upperworldly sense.

What is the well saying? It is not within the Telesterion, the conclusion of the sacred way. It is a grieving place. But it is also a resting place – a place to rest in grieving, a place where one's grieving can rest and go no further. One is tempted to stop here and go no further, no deeper. This is a compromise place, a place of hopelessness, of depression, and of anxiety – but also a place of comfort, where one can grieve and rest and grieve and rest. It is like being in the vicinity of one's virginity, sensing its echoes, as if it is enough to get that close and no closer. It is necessary to encounter this place; we may spend years in this place, moistening the body, getting in touch with the taste of salt, being drawn closer to the well, the depths of this experience. The decision to continue inward into the sanctuary is not ours, as architecturally it is the entrances to the sanctuary, the two propylaia, which are so oriented toward each other that they enhance the swaying rhythm of the procession. The movement deeper into the sanctuary is a severe experience; the way becomes narrower and darker, an entrance into a place of deep anxiety. What happens on the other side of the entrance to the sanctuary is mysterious; it is where Demeter's connection with Persephone in the Underworld takes place. The fear of this place is fear of rape, even though we do not need to imagine what went on in the sanctuary as a literal rape. Rather, this place embodies the consciousness of being taken over into Hades' realm.

The main portion of the sanctuary is the Telesterion, which is depressed into the ground. Like Demeter grieving at the loss of Persephone, one is taken into depression. Scully gives this description of the Telesterion:

> This building, after its Mycenaean beginnings, had at least five important enlargements from the very early archaic period onward during antiquity; but its essential character was always the same; a columned hall surrounded by windowless walls and pierced by narrow entrances. The mysteries were to take place inside, with the initiates crowded together by torchlight in a shadowy grove of columns.[3]

This solemn, mysterious, shadowy space intensifies the repetitious patterns of instinctual life. The action of virginizing intensifies the sensing body. We cannot look upon the transformation of the bond with the earth to the bond with the soul as one which leaves the body behind. It is, instead, an initiation *deeper* into the body, bringing together Demeter's earth body and Persephone's psychic body. But there is no transformation out of body.

Imagine initiates crowded together, the beams of their torches playing across the columns which are scattered like trees around the space of the sanctuary. The columns are stark, without fluting or design. The initiates dance around and around the columns, repeating in an intensified way the pattern begun at the outskirts of Athens. The initiates crowd the bank of steps around the interior walls. An instrument, the echeion, used to imitate thunder, is hit at the moment Persephone is called. But there is yet a further, more interior, more enclosed space, the Anaktoron, not exactly at the center but an interval between two rows of columns. The Anaktoron has a single entrance. To the right of it is the throne of the Hierophant — he who makes holy things appear. There is no decision to experience the body in this manner; the experience is simply brought to one, unexpectedly, like a clap of thunder, no matter how much preparation one has made. Plutarch likens philosophical illumination to what must happen in this space:

> Just as persons who are being initiated into the mysteries throng together at the outset amid tumult and shouting, and jostle against one another, but when the holy rites are being performed and disclosed the people are immediately attentive in awe and silence, so too at the beginning of philosophy; about its portals also you will see great tumult and talking and boldness, as some boorishly and violently try to jostle their way towards the repute it bestows; but he who has succeeded in getting inside, and has seen a great light, as though a shrine were opened, adopts another bearing of silence and amazement, and humbly and orderly attends upon reason as upon a god.[4]

Not philosophical illumination but initiation of psyche into the body and the body into psyche. The Anaktoron shines forth with light, not the light of illumination, but the light of fire. The journey into the sanctuary, culminating in the arrival at the Telesterion, is a repetitive passage into a more and more confined space in which instinctual life intensifies more and more; until there is no way out. One's own resources are taken away, and the body enters into a place where something is done to it. The place, the body, "flares up." A commentator on Aristotle's essay, *On Philosophy*, employs the term *eis phantasian* for what is produced in this space. And according to the Christian scholar Hippolytus, at the moment of thunder the Hierophant sings out: "The mistress has given birth to the holy boy, Brimo has given birth to Brimos! That is, the Strong one to the Strong one."[5]

What is born in this psychic space is phantasy, imaged as a child. The child is all sense, all body, the eternal child of the body, psychic body. Instinct now has someone to take care of, to attend to, and psyche has a place. Still, saying it this way smacks too much of an achievement, a goal. The stories of initiation into the Eleusinian Mysteries tell us that many went through the initiation more than once, emphasizing that the body is always on this labyrinthian, circular path; it never quite gets it once and for all.

Return now to the word *transformation*. The value of cultural psychology lies in its insistence that the language of psychology needs the substance of the world. Without that substantial sense, psychology becomes another spiritual trip. In the instance of virginity, one would always be looking for some illumination, some way out of the body. Virginity, I have been attempting to illustrate, concerns the movement of the instinctual body deeper into the body — one's own body and the body of the world.

1. Vincent Scully, *The Earth, The Temple, and the Gods* (New York: Praeger, 1969), p. 76.
2. Patricia Berry, "The Rape of Demeter/Persephone and Neurosis," in *Spring 1975* (New York: Spring Publications, 1975), p. 188.
3. Scully, p. 77.
4. Plutarch, *De Profectu in Virtute*, in *Moralia* with an English translation by Frank Cole Babbitt (Cambridge: Loeb Classical Library), I, p. 435.
5. Hippolytus, *The Refutation of All Heresies*, translated by Francis Legge (London and New York), I, p. 138.

The Virgin and the Unicorn

Tom Moore

On a warm, humid night not long ago, I was walking down Bourbon Street in New Orleans, passing by dusty antique taverns whining with homespun jazz and crowded creole restaurants advertised with buckets of oyster shells at their front doors. Spaced quite evenly between food and music on this street of pleasures in the city of sin were many varieties of sex shows. From the street I could see stout ladies quivering with fat on crude bar-runways and young men dressed in drag looking more feminine than their neighboring female competitors. At the doors of these sex palaces were hawkers trying to persuade passers-by to spend some time and money on one voyeur delight or another. As I approached one of these 'palaces' with a friend, the hawker called to us, with all the tempting lure he could grease into his voice: "Boys, you can't pass this by. Inside we have some fresh young virgins for you."

In a time when sex is 'big business,' virgins are the ultimate 'turn on.' In the film *Pretty Baby* (set in New Orleans, by the way), as in the stories of Marquis De Sade or the pseudo-biographical write-ups on the centerfolds of glossy 'skin' magazines, we find one of the cardinal rules of sex salesmanship: to fuel the enticement, make the object of fantasy a virgin. Since we are dealing here with voyeurism and not medieval virgin-testing, it is obvious that the attractions of the virgin are not physical. It is the *fantasy* of virginity that heightens the excitement and raises the price. Virginity itself has about it a seductive lure, an aura of attraction.

Although virgins are almost exclusively female in the 'business' of sex, virgin males may be equally alluring in other contexts. D.H. Lawrence once observed that "the greatest triumph an American woman can have is the triumph of seducing a man, especially if he is pure."[1] In my own early twenties, when I was an innocent, naive monk in a Catholic monastic order dedicated to the Virgin Mary—a young deer in the retinue of Artemis—my spiritual guides frequently warned me about women who enjoyed tracking virgin pelts like mine. Whether my advisors were entertaining some wishful thinking or visions of grandeur, their warnings are probably well-founded: virgins, whether male or female, are prized prey.

This image of the virgin is complicated, however, by archaic traditions attesting to a deep fear of virgins. Early anthropologists came back from the field with accounts of children deflowered even before the age of puberty, or of husbands protected from the dangers involved in the defloration of their wives by the beneficent mediation of a professional 'deflorator,' a priest or lord. The much-contested history of the medieval practice, *jus primae noctis* — "the right of the first night" — gained evidence from these anthropologists. But modern authors, influenced as they are by the pleasant fantasy of the virgin's lure, seem to have trouble appreciating the horror involved in deflowering a virgin. Wolfgang Lederer, for example, in his strange book *The Fear of Women*, alludes to an oriental practice of employing men of some fortitude to deflower virgins. He comments rather sarcastically: "We cannot help but envy them their courage."[2]

In order to understand its enticement, we must explore the perils which virginity entails, both literally, in encounters between people where virginity is a factor, and in the wider sense of "virginal." We need also to consider the problem that arises when one avoids, or simply does not see, the danger in the virgin. And in this rather complicated matter we may ask: is the virgin's mischievous tendency to threaten and wound her shadow? or is the shadow already contained in the virgin's own innocence and sweetness?

Soft Hands on the Unicorn Shaft

A fuller picture of the alluring virgin, as well as an answer to some of these questions, is suggested in the tale of the unicorn. In Western tradition, the unicorn's existence as an imaginary beast can be traced at least as far back as pre-Christian Greece.[3] The Christian Church Fathers offer some significant comparisons and interpretations of the animal, but the basic story is told in an anonymous text, from approximately the third century A.D., known as the *Physiologus*. This book, quite popular during the Middle Ages, was translated and adapted many times, resulting in several variations of the unicorn image. The unicorn is also well known as the subject of a series of tapestries at Cluny in France, and at The Cloisters in New York. Jung also devoted a section of *Psychology and Alchemy* to the unicorn.[4]

Though something of a grotesque anomaly in the animal world, the unicorn is quite an attractive beast. He is usually depicted as horse-like — all-white in color and, of course, topped with a magnificent single horn which is either curved, or straight and spiraling. Old texts warn that this beast is ferociously wild and cannot be captured alive. The only way to take a unicorn is to place a virgin in his vicinity.

> When a man intends to hunt it [the unicorn], and to take it and ensnare it, he goes to the forest where is its repair, there he places a virgin, with her breast uncovered, and by its scent the unicorn perceives it; then it comes to the virgin and kisses her breast, falls asleep on her lap and so comes to its death. The man arrives immediately and kills it in its sleep...or takes it alive.[5]

The complete image of the unicorn and the virgin, then, includes deception and death. These are factors to be explored after looking more closely at the unicorn himself.

With his long stiff horn, the unicorn is doubtless a phallic symbol. Of course the beast is much more than that, but we should not dismiss, in an attitude of impatience with Freud and his ever-present phallic images, this evident aspect. The unicorn is clearly masculine; he has a great capacity for carnage and violence and he possesses penetrating power, approaching the feminine erect and fertile. But there are countless kinds of phalli and many methods of fertilizing; a more specific aspect of the unicorn's phallic power is suggested by Rilke's description of the horn: "like a steeple on the moon."[6]

The unicorn's single horn is related to the deer's antlers, to stately Artemis *Orthia* ("the upright"), and to the heights of mountains where the highly spiritual God of Judaism appears – where the spiritual master, Christ, preached his creed, and the guru offers spiritual guidance.[7] The unicorn is a spiritual beast, or more precisely, the beastliness of spirit. Jung at one point identifies the unicorn as the "spermatic word or spirit,"[8] while elsewhere he relates the unicorn to the "angry moodiness," the violent side of Yahweh. "Like this irritable beast," says Jung, Yahweh "reduced the world to chaos and could only be moved to love in the lap of a pure virgin."[9] According to St. Albert the Great, it was the unicorn that drove Adam and Eve from Eden, destroyed the world with a great flood, and annihilated the Sodomites with hellfire and brimstone.[10]

Although the unicorn is often depicted as a gentle beast, he appears occasionally as violent and dangerous. In the fourth tapestry of the Cloisters series, for example, the unicorn is shown wounding a dog with his sharp pointed horn. This ferocity is an image of spirit. Spirit is often romanticized in glorious religious fantasies, but, as Jung argued in many of his writings (especially in his book on Job), there is also a violent, destructive, threatening side to spirit. I have heard serious students of Tibetan Buddhism warn against the easy Americanization of Tibetan spiritual practices, precisely out of respect for the ravages of spirit. When spiritual devotion leads a person to fast until death, when the spirit of the times is voiced with muscle in a McCarthyism of purges and purifications, and even when the spirit of an academic discipline treats the imagination as if it were a threatening contamination, we sense the sharp point of the spirit. The steeple turned on its side becomes a potent weapon.

Spirit quickens and impregnates the psyche with fantasy and movement, nourishing the soul. Traditionally the unicorn horn was a priceless prize that could, for example, purify water poisoned by snakes. Pieces of unicorn horn were placed in drinking vessels to prevent political poisonings. The horn was commonly used to advertise apothecary shops – a source of good health. It was even used as an aphrodisiac.

The benefits of spirit are quite apparent; it is its beastly, menacing side that, strangely, often goes unnoticed. Marsilio Ficino aptly located the place of psychological consciousness as lying midway between body and spirit. The soul, he claimed, has an affection for both the body and the spirit, but it can thrive only at a mid-point between them. Soul can lean too much towards the body or towards the spirit.[11]

In *Psychology and Alchemy*, Jung reprints a picture from alchemical texts showing a confrontation between a stag and a unicorn.[12] The original text identifies the stag as soul and the unicorn as spirit. The stag, with its tall antlers, represents that part or phase of the soul, quite spiritual in itself, as it comes to grips with the mighty, pointed spirit of the unicorn, whose horn has no branches, no differentiation. The Church Fathers associated the unicorn's horn with the monotheistic Father: spirit become so high, focused, and sharp-pointed as to be quite dangerous. The unicorn presents us with an image of the problem which soul has with spirit. Knowing its amazing, magically beneficial properties as well as its potential for destruction, how does soul deal with spirit? Or, in slightly different terms, how do we deal with spirit psychologically? How do we approach, for example, spiritual practices and religious concerns without neglecting soul? How do we carry on our intellectual work and even our theorizing about psychology without loss of soul? And, conversely, how do we care for the soul – while engaging in psychotherapy, for instance – without becoming lost in the body and its problems of daily life?

The answer given in the long-standing story of the unicorn is that we have to entice spirit with the virginal. The unicorn cannot be taken alive in any other way. We may get hold of spirit in action and in religious ritual (actually it often gets hold of us, even though we tend to think otherwise), or we may grasp it, at least fleetingly, in abstraction. In the first case, however, we are destroyed psychologically, trampled to death – like Hippolytus – by the force of the spirit that has taken us over. In the second case, the spirit evaporates by the fire of intellectual inquiry and is dissipated in the winds of scholarly discussion. The only way to get hold of spirit and soul *together* is to lure the unicorn into the virgin's temenos, her "enclosed special place," and then into her lap, where the beast nurses at her breast (according to some versions) and impregnates her. *The virginal nourishes the spirit, while spirit makes the virginal psyche pregnant.*

This virginal psyche which lures spirit may take the form of a new attitude, a fresh perspective, a new image, or even a familiar image freshly imagined. Ficino followed the Hermetic tradition which held that images, like statues and amulets, could attract the spirit of the planets and stars. He called images "magic decoys" for luring spirit.[13] Imagination vivifies because it draws spirit to itself. Spirit and body meet within the uterine confines of a virginal image, so that body becomes spirited and spirit is incarnated – given limit, shape, and personality. Incarnated in an image, spirit no longer appears as a vague mood or a faceless sense of urgency. The compulsion of the spirit is tamed in the lap of a virginal image; it is given a face. In one of the tapestries from Cluny, the virgin holds a mirror up to the face of the unicorn, reflecting his image.

While a captured spirit gives our images life, a virgin image also nourishes spirit. The unicorn nurses at the virgin's breast. She gives of her special milk:[14] *lac virginis*, "virgin's milk," a lotion used to keep the skin clear and smooth. It keeps the psychic body, our imagery, fresh. Spirit needs to be removed from the ethereal element, where human breath is stifled, and brought into the more elemental mixture – the humid sphere of virgin's milk, for example, or her womb, or her garden.

In his seminal essay on virginity, John Layard suggests that the virginal psyche does not allow introjections from the outside – all those things we *should* think and see, as they are pointed out to us by parents, teachers, authorities, or even good archetypal psychologists. The virginal psyche is innocent, unknowing, and untutored in such expectations and limitations. In other words, the virginal psyche reflects the complexity of spiritual matters: no simplifications, no adjustments to favored styles of thought and expression, no symbolic shorthand. As in the virginal reflection of dreams, learning and logic have no place in the virginal psyche.

Layard also describes projections as a violation of the virginal, but here we have to make some distinctions. For example, fantasies which we bring to a situation or even to a relationship may still be virginal. They may be the compulsive, unconscious, and unreflective 'acting out' of the spirit that violates the virginity of the psyche. In such acting out, spirit has no containment, no psychic body. With the full force of its violent destructive power, spirit may be unleashed in murderous action. The newspapers are full of stories of spirit taking possession, whether in a murder involving a love triangle, or in a slug-out between a football coach and an opposing player. Afterward, people say: "I don't know what came over me."

The alternative to unreflective behavior is not, however, simply to hold on blindly to the virginal image. The unicorn tapestries do not end with a tableau of the virgin grasping the horn. Once captured, the unicorn is given over to the hunters, who have been waiting in ambush as if all along they had been part of the virgin's snare. The hunters kill the unicorn by plunging their spears into his white body. There is something devious in the virgin's lure.

Incarnation, Passion, and Resurrection

Psychological concern with spirit requires more than just its capture and containment; our exploration of further imaginal development will entail a look at other mythic images and divine persons connected with spirit, unicorns, and virgins. We know, not through the unicorn tapestries but from a number of paintings which explicitly show the unicorn as a double of the Holy Spirit overshadowing the virgin, that the unicorn is involved in the Virgin Mother's conception. Jung reprints a picture in which the unicorn, in the lap of the virgin, stands beneath a beam of light descending from the Holy Spirit and shining on the virgin's womb.[15] Within the *hortus conclusus* – the "enclosed garden" – of the virgin shown in many representations of this scene, the unicorn is a spirit made flesh. The Church Fathers identified this unicorn with Christ. Tertullian writes: "Christ is meant by this animal, and the horn denotes Christ's cross."[16] St. Ambrose makes the same connection, and St. Basil calls Christ the son of unicorns, describing the unicorn as "irresistible in might and unsubjected to man."[17] In a ninth-century version of the *Physiologus*, we find: "In this way Our Lord Jesus Christ, the spiritual unicorn, descended into the womb of the virgin and through her took on human flesh."[18]

The entire story of Christian redemption is told in the fate of the unicorn: incarnation, passion and death, and resurrection. The unicorn's attraction to the virgin is presented in the imagery of the Annunciation – the conception of the child within the virgin's womb. The unicorn's suffering and death parallel Christ's passion and crucifixion. Finally, in the last of the Cloisters tapestries, the unicorn, like Christ, is resurrected, and stands within a fenced circle.

In order to get deeper into the image of suffering and death, we have to consider yet another parallel: the mythic image of the young hunter Actaeon who encounters the virgin goddess Artemis at her virginal bath deep in the woods. Because he beholds her utter nakedness, he is lacerated and killed by his own hunting dogs. The image of Actaeon is particularly significant, for it shows an interaction between two archetypal patterns. In Actaeon's story, Artemis is allied with the life-giving, death-dealing god Dionysus.[19] Some of the Dionysian elements in Actaeon's fate are circumstantial: they were cousins; Pentheus, another victim of Dionysian dismemberment, was also a cousin, and he was killed on the same mountain as Actaeon. More significantly, Actaeon suffered the typical Dionysian fate of dismemberment—*sparagmos*. Finally, in the Christian tradition, Christ is identified not only with the unicorn but also with Actaeon.

Even the virgin mother of Jesus experiences an Actaeonic passion. The innocent young virgin becomes the "Mother of Sorrows" whose *Via Dolorosa* extends from the infancy of her son to his death and burial. The hopeful and glorious conception and birth, celebrated today at Christmas with fantasies of moral purity, peace, and hope, lead to a life of suffering for the mother; the depiction in religious art of her heart pierced by swords must call to mind the piercing of Actaeon, of Jesus, and of the unicorn. In another image that fascinated medieval and Renaissance artists and sculptors, the sorrowful virgin holds the broken body of her son as it is lowered from the cross — the Pietà. The unicorn's power has become wounded and flaccid in the lap of the virgin.[20]

The unicorn, along with Actaeon and Jesus, leads us to consider the Dionysian pathology that accompanies psychological virginity. Once incarnated and reflected in the purity of thought and imagination, an image is exposed to a variety of thoughts and experiences waiting in ambush. When spirit is caught in a new idea or embodied in a fresh vocabulary, a different style of life, or a change in profession or locale, it succumbs eventually to the hunters who, lying in wait, attack it and test it, so that it is deepened with the very contamination and pain which they bring. Virgin fantasy and imagining invite deepening by the god of dismemberment and death; indeed, they require it. At the concrete level, we may see this deepening either as a ripening of the soul, a maturing in character and awareness, or as the effects which the Dionysian elements can have upon the image itself. Our virgin ideas, at first so pure and promising, are crucified. The vessels of spirit are dismembered, as Freud's once virgin-fresh theories were minced by Norman O. Brown and others, or as Jung's have been 'contaminated' and 'lacerated' by Hillman, Lopez-Pedraza, and their cohorts. The purity of the virginal imagery is adulterated and simultaneously deepened by the deathly touch of Dionysian immorality and abandon. Of course, the virginal language and images of Hillman and Lopez-Pedraza also face a Dionysian future.

But the story of the unicorn is still incomplete; we have not fully considered the last tapestry until we behold the resurrected unicorn. After death his vitality is restored, though he is now tame, content to rest within the perimeters of a circular fence, an emblem of the virginal membrane. The virgin does not now entice with milk; she simply contains. If these three phases—lure and conception, passion and death, and resurrection—are seen not as sequential stages necessarily but as three dimensions of psyche's dealings with spirit, then we may say that the virginal freshness of our imagining is never fully destroyed by the Dionysian element. The virginal survives and thrives through the Dionysian. Jung's insights, his immaculate ideas and images, are not destroyed by a seemingly rebel scion called archetypal psychology; they remain intact, though deepened by his successors. The virgin's lure and bait may well appear as shadow – hunters waiting in ambush, waiting to attack – but her enticement is finally revealed as a necessity, a quickening of imagination. In Dionysus, the pregnancy of the virgin is brought to term. Artemis, though virgin, was the patroness of childbirth.

Therapists are familiar with the process of redeeming images. A dream may show the bath in which virginity is renewed. It may take place in the bathroom or shower, or in a more religious setting – in a deep underground pool, or at a pond in the woods. The dreamer, presumably, is ready to give body to some new spirit. Or, something is said in therapy—a new idea, a fresh insight—that fills the patient with feelings of promise and excitement. This is but a beginning, an immaculate conception—a conception in pleasure, as in the story of Eros and Psyche – in which the psyche is made pregnant. The image is then hunted down by the vicissitudes of life: attacked, pierced, killed. But, as usual, death and the pain of life are revealed as the servants of depth, and in this way the image survives, reflected even more deeply in virginal imagination.

The Virgin's Shadow

Dionysian dismemberment is no joke, even though some of our best unicorn hunters are comedians. Humor and comic mockery attack our sacred ideas – and their embodiments in the form of institutions – without annihilating them. Though filled with life, Dionysian experience is also saturated with death and the pain of falling apart. Therefore, it is not unusual to find that the Dionysian is avoided in favor of long dalliance with the virgin. If Dionysian falling apart and susceptibility to attack are pathologies of the virginal psyche, then its shadow emerges in the avoidance of these pathologies.

The genuine danger in virginal consciousness is not the invitation to Dionysian disruption and suffering. Quite the opposite: the virgin's real threat is the paralysis and implosive power which she inflicts upon those who linger in her pleasures and become devoted exclusively to her. Hippolytus is an example of youthful spirit so taken with virginal imagery and ideals that he is undone by his own haughtiness, his exalted sense of purity, and his exaggerated confidence in his own idealism and conviction. Those who remain fixed upon their ideals and visions, allowing no attack and no development, are also children of the virgin.[21] They are not only moral puritans but also intellectual purists who require that their ideas, vocabularies, and systems of thought remain as intact as on the day they were conceived. Whether in therapy or not, they are tempted by the virgin to dally with fascinating and promising dreams and images, for they are unwilling to give up the virgin's breast and submit to that Dionysian riot.

The problem with the virgin's shadow is that it is so bright, white, and spanking clean. One feels righteous – again like Hippolytus – if one stands on the side of the virgin. In therapy, the analyst may feel like the spoiler, deflowering the virgin patient time after time. Educators, too, see this virgin shadow constellated when they present their students with exciting ideas. If the students put off the Dionysian pathology, so central to learning, in the name of purity and thought, the teacher becomes the professional 'deflorator,' provided he is not himself a servant of the virgin.

The image of the virgin grasping the unicorn's splendid horn, which appears so often in medieval and Renaissance illustrations, reminds us of the highly spiritual quality of the virgin's shadow. If soul is lost in virginal consciousness, it is lost in the spirit, in the upper reaches of intellectual and moral purity. Spiritual purity may impede psychological development.

A striking example of such a spiritual dominion – the Oneida Community of upstate New York – leads us back to concrete instances of virginity. John Humphrey Noyes founded this religious commune during the middle of the nineteenth century.[22] Noyes was a principled man, fully committed to living the gospel of Jesus (as he interpreted it), and his followers, some four hundred at one time in Oneida, appear to have been equally devout in their religious practices. They were called "Perfectionists," and their many writings often included advice about remaining pure of heart and keeping a clear conscience. What was remarkable about this Christian community was its literal interpretation of the New Testament claim that there would be no marriage in the kingdom of heaven. Noyes was an early advocate of "realized eschatology" – the idea that the kingdom which Jesus preached has already come – and he therefore replaced the traditional monogamous marriage with what he called the "complex marriage." Under this system, all members of the community were considered partners of a single marriage, and they had sexual relationships with each other freely and in good conscience. Noyes developed a system that encouraged older folks in the commune to have sexual relations with the younger people, but he would not under any circumstance allow emotional entanglements between two individuals. He established a practice of "mutual criticism," a sort of encounter session, in which couples showing signs of enduring affection for each other would be advised to change their ways. If a couple could not or would not alter their mutual affections, one of them would be sent off to another branch of the community, preferably in another state. Noyes himself took care of the virgins' 'first night,' which for him and his family was a spiritual act. The spiritual nature of this sexual arrangement is evident in the dissolution of the experiment. Local theologians finally applied so much pressure against the 'immoral' commune that Noyes finally abandoned his leadership and moved on. His successor, who regarded the commune as a social experiment, lacked Noyes' religious and theological sensitivity, with the result that first the "complex marriage" and finally the commune itself fell apart.

What is particularly revealing in this example is the Perfectionists' systematic attempt, not to avoid the body, but to suppress the soul. The atmosphere of commune life combined religious fervor with a purity and paranoia common to spiritual groups. Spiritual clarity was their highest goal which, when translated into principles at the human level, required freedom from intimate, personal entanglements. One individual sent away for his sin of affection wrote: "I desire your prayers that I... be not again entangled in the yoke of bondage."[23] In 1866, the commune's newsletter, *The Daily Journal*, expressed the commune's atmosphere in this way:

> There seems to be a bright, joyous spirit prevailing in the family. Since the departure of our last Hadean ambassador, the spiritual atmosphere is a great deal clearer.[24]

Could this ambassador from Hades have been one of its proper residents – Dionysus?

Emotion, entanglement, jealousy, and individuality – significant marks of the psychological – were all excluded from Oneida. "Complex marriage" was actually an attempt to render relationships simple, spiritually neat and pure. Individual reflection and exploration were replaced by loyalty to a spiritual leader – a phenomenon we still find in contemporary religious cults. In fact, the tendency to avoid the complexity, the mess and dirt, and the imperfections of life in its particularity and instability goes hand-in-hand with a desire to replace the individual person by a higher, more spiritual figure of fantasy. Whether it appears projected upon a living person – an historical, religious, or other figure – or within psychological analysis and theory, this aloof fantasy figure may well signal the virgin's shadow.

Fear of Virgins

We end up, then, with two quite different reasons for suggesting why virgins might be feared – why husbands, for instance, are protected from the dangers of deflowering their brides. One reason is that virginity is an invitation to a long, painful working out of ideas and fantasies in life. The other reason, feared only by those who see the shadow in the blazing pure light, is that the virgin tends to put a lock on her "enclosed garden" – a kind of chastity belt of the imagination – which keeps one distant from the vitality, as well as the pain, of Dionysian life. Still, the fear of virgins calls for further elaboration.

Freud, who was interested in the threat posed by the virgin, explored the problem with an essay entitled "The Taboo of Virginity."[25] He associated the taboo with the traditional fear of blood, and, by inference, with the more general taboo against murder. Elaborating on Freud, we can reflect on the potential violence and destructiveness inherent in a virginal mentality, which by definition is untutored in the mores and morals of civilized life. Perhaps in this sense, the Dionysian flows so easily from the virginal; the cruelty which children sometimes manifest may be but the dark side of their uncultivated innocence.

Freud's own psychoanalytic explanation for the taboo against virgins is rather intricate, but it illuminates yet another aspect of virginal consciousness. The reason the husband might fear his virgin wife, says Freud, is, first, that she suffers a 'narcissistic wound' with the loss of her physical virginity – she has given up once and for all something valuable and protected; therefore, although she may love her husband, she will also resent his deed. Second, since she has long been deeply attached to her father, or perhaps to a brother, she will be disappointed with her first sexual experience, since her husband can never match her fantasies of love for her father.

Freud's suggestion leads us to reflect upon the virgin's preference for an exalted fantasy, as opposed to any concrete image, any individual, in life. Such a virginal attitude holds on to fantasies larger than life, avoiding the paltry situations and personalities that life brings. Confronting a psychological virgin, the ordinary mortal might well feel rather insignificant, and in this way he might experience the force of the taboo against penetrating that membrane. Once again, incidentally, we see how puer psychology is enclosed within virginal consciousness: Puer, too, exhibits the same haughtiness, ambition, voyeurism, idealism, and purity.

There would seem to be three possible responses to this excessively virginal attitude. If we were to deal with someone in whom the virgin's shadow was constellated, we might enter the virgin's enclosed circle (in an academic setting, for example, we might learn to speak its language and adopt its assumptions); or, we might become the ravager and spoiler, even at the risk of the virgin's resentment and furor (a scenario which Freud rightly depicted); or, if both virgin and 'other' were willing to assent to the demands of life, they might together enjoy this primal intercourse—deepening and preserving, all the same, the virginal reality. This third response holds the promise of a virgin birth — the unfolding and intensifying of insight, for example, or the birth of an image without loss of its virginity.

The virgin's penchant for exalted fantasy is evidenced by the custom of substituting a less personal, more imaginary figure for the husband in the act of defloration. At Oneida, too, Noyes was not truly an individual human being deflowering his virgins: he was bigger than life—a spiritual leader, a prophet, and a father equal to the fantasy of the virgins. His act did not really deflower them psychologically. Some of his virgins may have become pregnant in body, but none in psyche. In Jungian and archetypal psychology, we face the dangerous temptation of becoming Oneidians, leaving Jung, Hillman, Plato, or some Greek deity to do our work for us. In so doing we remain pure and virginal; but, by avoiding life, we commit Hippolytus' crime of monotheism—except that in our case the god whom we neglect is Dionysus. When, in this purist attitude, we avoid individual persons and situations by calling on archetypal images, not as instruments for seeing through the individual and concrete situation, but as psychological *jus primae noctis*, as substitutes, we make our archetypal work monotheistic, a service to the virgin alone. In therapy, for example, when we substitute archetypal patterns for specific dream images — seeing a shadow in the dream, for instance, and then dealing with the idea of shadow rather than with the image—we are inviting a John Humphrey Noyes to take over what should be our own work and pleasure.

An imaginal viewpoint that avoids the virgin's shadow will perceive the imaginal dimension of the concrete; such an attitude can be *in* life while not *of* it: that is, not literal. The fully virginal-Dionysian perspective demands that one believe in the virgin birth of images and in their resurrection. Images may be born into life without literalism, and they may be submitted to deadly though deepening life without annihilation. In this way, the unicorn, or spirit, attains a resting place within the circular fence—enticed by fresh imagination, it suffers the wounds of life and is resurrected in reflection.

1. Quoted in Elizabeth Hardwick, *Seduction and Betrayal: Women and Literature* (New York: Vintage Books, 1975), p. 189.
2. Wolfgang Lederer, *The Fear of Women* (New York: Harcourt Brace Jovanovich, Inc., 1968), p. 44.
3. Ctesias, a Greek physician of the fifth century, B.C., wrote about the unicorn in his book, *Indica*. On this and for a well-documented, finely illustrated study of the unicorn, see Margaret B. Freeman, *The Unicorn Tapestries* (New York: The Metropolitan Museum of Art, 1976).
4. See C.G. Jung, *Collected Works*, XII, trans. R.F.C. Hull, Bollingen Series XX (Princeton: Princeton University Press, 1968), Ch. 6.
5. Quoted in Freeman, p. 21, from Thomas Wright, *Popular Treatises on Science Written during the Middle Ages* (London, 1841), p. 81.
6. See Rilke's "Das Einhorn," in *Sämtliche Werke*, I (Wiesbaden: Insel-Verlag, 1955), pp. 506–07; the poem is discussed in Rüdiger Rober Beer, *Unicorn: Myth and Reality*, trans. Charles M. Stern (New York: Mason-Charter, 1977), pp. 157–58.
7. For more on the imagery of antlers, horns, and heights, see my essay "Artemis and the Puer," in *Puer Papers*, ed. James Hillman (Irving: Spring Publications, 1979); also Hillman, "Peaks and Vales," in *On the Way to Self-Knowledge*, ed. Jacob Needleman and Dennis Lewis (New York: Alfred A. Knopf, 1976), reprinted in *Puer Papers*.
8. Jung, *Collected Works*, V, § 492.
9. Jung, *Collected Works*, XI, § 259.
10. Quoted in Beer, p. 80.
11. Those of us who study these things are usually careful about losing soul in the body, but perhaps we especially are less aware of the dangers of spirit.
12. Jung, *Collected Works*, XII, § 240.
13. In the first chapter of *De Vita Coelitus Comparanda*, Ficino describes the relationship between the World Soul and material images: "These kinds of forms, corresponding to 'ratios' of the World Soul, Zoroaster called Divine Allurements, and Synesius confirmed that they are 'magic decoys.' He truly believed that everything at a certain time draws gifts right from the soul to a certain proper material species."
14. On a related image of milk, see Hillman, "Senex and Puer: An Aspect of the Historical and Psychological Present," in *Eranos Jahrbuch* 36 (Zürich: Rhein, 1969), pp. 343–48, reprinted in *Puer Papers*.
15. Jung, *Collected Works* V, plate VIII, "The Overshadowing of Mary," painting on wood, Erfurt Cathedral, pp. 1620–40.
16. Quoted in Freeman, p. 17, from "Adversus Marcionem."
17. *Ibid.*, from "Homily on Psalm 28."
18. *Ibid.*, p. 19.
19. For a development of this Dionysian factor in the Actaeon image, see my essay "Artemis and the Puer," in *Puer Papers*.
20. Walter Spinks, *The Axis of Eros* (New York: Penguin Books, 1973), p. 9.
21. On the difference between a 'child' of a God and his 'follower,' or the difference between being exclusively fixed in an archetypal pattern and consciously acknowledging it, see Rafael Lopez-Pedraza, *Hermes and His Children* (New York: Spring Publications, 1977), p. 119.

22. For a sketch of the Oneida experience which clearly depicts Noyes as the spiritual leader of the community, see Maren Lockwood Carden, *Oneida: Utopian Community to Modern Corporation* (New York: Harper and Row, 1971).

23. *Daily Journal* (Oneida Community). Vol. 2, No. 121, p. 483.

24. *Ibid.*, No. 99, p. 381. A recent study of a fourteenth-century French community also demonstrates the extraordinary role of the religious leader in sexual matters. Pierre Clergue, a priest, deflowered a virgin, then had her married off. After the marriage she continued to have sexual relations with the priest. The husband knew about it: "Sometimes he would ask me: 'Has the priest done it with you?' And I would answer: 'Yes.' And my husband would say: 'As far as the priest is concerned all right! But don't you go having other men.' " See Le Roy Ladurie, *Montaillou: The Promised Land of Error* (New York: George Braziller, 1978), p. 158.

25. Sigmund Freud, *Collected Papers*, IV, trans. Joan Riviere (New York: Basic Books, 1959), pp. 217-35.

"For Ever Wilt Thou Love, and She Be Fair" Faulkner's Image of Virginity

Louise Cowan

In *Go Down, Moses*, a novel about two-thirds of the way through his writing career, William Faulkner for the first time explores the full implication of a theme that may well bear the major burden of his entire body of work. It is the theme of non-consummation, of not seizing that which one has the opportunity to seize. His concern centers on the young Isaac McCaslin, who, when he is able to shoot the legendary bear Old Ben, for some obscure reason holds his fire. Later, his cousin-counselor McCaslin Edmonds attempts to make him understand his own motives. Taking a book down from the shelf, Cass opens it and turns to the boy:

> "Listen," he said. He read the five stanzas aloud and closed the book on his finger and looked up. "All right," he said, "Listen" and read again, but only one stanza this time and closed the book and laid it on the table. "She cannot fade, though thou hast not thy bliss," McCaslin said: "Forever wilt thou love, and she be fair."
>
> "He's talking about a girl," the boy said.
>
> "He had to talk about something," McCaslin said. Then he said, "He was talking about truth. Truth is one. It doesn't change. It covers all things which touch the heart.... Do you see now?"[1]

In reading Keats' "Ode on a Grecian Urn" to Isaac, Cass is making an appeal to the boy's imagination, attempting to lead him beyond a literal sense of his own life. He draws upon a poem central to Faulkner's work, one that echoes throughout the texture and tonality of his language and recurs as overt image and phrase in *Sartoris, Light in August,* and *The Mansion,* as well as *Go Down, Moses.* Keats' poem depicts a "still unravished bride of quietness," a witness who though mute can yet "tell a flowery tale." The urn, too, like Cass and Keats, speaks in figures, not precepts: it depicts, at least in the stanza Cass repeats, a scene of music and love. But the melodies are "unheard" by us; and the love is unconsummated by the lover, "though winning near the kiss." The young man pursuing his beloved is nevertheless enjoined not to grieve. In failing to achieve his goal, he will be spared the pangs of a "heart high sorrowful and cloyed, / A burning forehead and a parching tongue." The passion in which he participates, given form by the artist at its highest moment, is "far above" all "breathing human passion." It has been lifted into timelessness, into transcendence; his love and the beauty of his beloved will endure. "Forever," the poet assures him, "wilt thou love and she be fair."

The truth that lies behind what Cass is trying to teach Isaac in interpreting his "not shooting" is that the way to possess the beloved object is to renounce it – to allow it to keep its virginity. This attitude requires what John Layard calls the "internalisation through sacrifice,"[2] that "passion week of the heart," as Faulkner has elsewhere described it,[3] in which the heart suffers its own immolation. In refraining from the act of possessing what one desires, Faulkner seems to say, one moves to a higher and more perfect act: contemplation and love. This passion of desire and abnegation is the concern of all Faulkner's fiction – his figure in the carpet, so to speak – to which he addressed himself throughout his career. The constitutive elements of his "figure," for which the "Ode on a Grecian Urn" is ikon, are all images of virginity – the fleeing maiden, the desiring but unattaining suitor, and finally the urn itself, the "unravished bride" which, embracing both lover and beloved, bestows itself most intensely and yet remains whole and undivided, witnessing to the integrity of truth and beauty, becoming a dispassionate "friend to man." Under the governance of such a paradigm, apparently separate themes and motifs in Faulkner's body of work are gathered up in a vision of desire and renunciation, of eros and agape, of crucifixion and resurrection. Like Keats, Faulkner perceives this essentially Judaeo-Christian insight in a classically Greek form, his imagination shedding on the ordinary life about him the light of antiquity.

When his focus is on the masculine figure caught up in this pattern of abnegation and sacrifice, Faulkner portrays him as the lover, either forever yearning in an anguish of unfulfillment or partaking of an immolation so complete as to transcend the ordinary boundaries of selfhood. The feminine aspect of the configuration – the yearned-for ideal – is portrayed as either the almost boyish Artemis or the fertile and alluring Aphrodite. Both feminine figures are unattainable; both are virginal.

And though the abnegation in this constellation of symbols is assigned to the masculine and the ambiguous elusiveness to the feminine, it is more accurate to say that the virginal, in its fulness, is beyond gender. It is the urn, the "enclosed garden" which in the midst of a fallen world contains both the wholeness of Eden and the consummation of the New Jerusalem. The Grecian urn contains both lover and beloved, caught in time and transformed into timelessness. Thus for Faulkner the image of virginity consists of not only the perpetually desirable maiden but the untouched primordial wilderness, the innocent purity of a boy, the seasoned wisdom of a celibate. These are all aspects of a quality and a power which man has misconstrued or forgotten.

Isaac McCaslin maintains his Edenic innocence long into old age, as evidenced by his remark to the group of young men accompanying him on his final hunting trip: speaking of the holiness of love, he says, "when a man and woman, at the instant when it dont even matter whether they marry or not, I think that whether they marry then or afterward or dont never, at that instant the two of them together were God." (p. 348)

"Then there are some Gods in this world I wouldn't want to touch and with a damn long stick," Roth Edmonds says. "And that includes myself, if you want to know," he adds. (p. 348) Roth's indictment of himself is based on a bitter awareness of his failure to love, in the cruel advantage he has taken of a girl who loves him, a young woman of mixed blood distantly related to the black side of the McCaslin dynasty. The other young men, however, seem touched by the old man's testimony. After Roth has left the room, they stand around Uncle Isaac, not meeting his eyes but drawn to him, "apparently held there yet by his quiet and peaceful voice as the heads of the swimming horses had been held above the water by his weightless hand." (p. 348) They sense even if they do not understand his inner strength, which stems from a passionate commitment made when, as a boy, he was initiated into the hunt by the old Indian half-breed Sam Fathers.

It is a singleness and integrity of heart that Isaac has been taught by his mentor, who inculcates in him a love and respect for the wilderness, the old wild untamed "still unravished bride of quietness." Sam Fathers, himself a celibate, chooses, after his task of teaching the boy is over, to live in the big woods, undisturbed by any human attachment – except for his participation in the annual hunt, the "yearly pageant-rite of the old bear's furious immortality." (p. 194) As Cass explains to Isaac when the boy expresses his dismay at Sam's desire to become a hermit, Sam is like an old lion or a bear in a cage who, born in captivity, suddenly one day smells the jungle. Afterwards he cannot escape the smell of the cage:

> "He hadn't smelled the cage until that minute. Then the hot sand or the brake blew into his nostrils and blew away, and all he could smell was the cage. That's what makes his eyes look like that."
>
> "Then let him go!" the boy cried. "Let him go!"
>
> His cousin laughed shortly. Then he stopped laughing... "His cage aint McCaslins," he said. "He was a wild man. When he was born, all his blood on both sides, except for the little white part, knew things that had been tamed out of our blood so long ago that we have not only forgotten them, we have to live together in herds to protect ourselves from our own sources." (p. 167)

Civilized people, Cass here implies, must protect themselves not only from the impenetrable darkness of pre-tribal existence where panic alone is the protector of fragile mortality, but from something more deeply buried than even the instinctual. They must protect themselves from the primal innocence itself, that innocence and wholeness of the Garden, possessed by man before Eve was separated from Adam, a memory of blessedness that civilization progressively destroys. Isaac McCaslin as a boy had demonstrated this innocence when he followed in the track of the old bear, renouncing gun and compass and watch.

General Compson says of him to the assembled company, including Cass:

> "...this boy was already an old man long before you damned Sartorises and Edmondses invented farms and banks to keep

> yourselves from having to find out what this boy was born knowing and fearing too maybe but without being afraid, that could go ten miles on a compass because he wanted to look at a bear none of us had ever got near enough to put a bullet in and looked at the bear and came the ten miles back on the compass in the dark; maybe by God that's the why and wherefore of farms and banks." (p. 251)

Compson has hit upon the "why and wherefore of farms and banks" – the very *raison d'etre* of human culture. This sustaining energy, the cause of civilization, lies in the psychic pattern of action in which the boy participates: an action at once passionate and restrained, erotic and ascetic. In his yearning to look upon sacred mystery, he has had the desire and the courage to pursue the numinous as well as the respect and love to refrain from conquering it. This action – one that, as General Compson implies, regenerates society – is most fittingly performed in a realm which, not being cultivated by man, maintains its virginal integrity.

Hence, though Isaac McCaslin later marries, and possesses for a while that "brief unsubstanced glory" (not lasting, Faulkner says, and "hence why glory"), the woods will always be "his mistress and his wife," (p. 326) the presence through which transcendence is to be encountered. Assembled, then, in this parable of death and rebirth are the virginal wilderness, the solitude, the loneliness, "through which frail and timorous man had merely passed without altering it, leaving no mark or scar" (p. 202); the celibate bear "so long unwifed and childless as to have become its own ungendered progenitor" (p. 210); the dedicated boy; and his teacher, the anchorite of the wilderness, Sam Fathers. The boy knows that the bear must someday be killed. "That's why it must be one of us," (p. 363) he says to Sam. And by one of us he means an initiate, someone with a virginal heart, whose love for a reality higher than himself has surmounted his own limitations, has transformed *eros*, so that it breaks through to that primal love in the image of which man was created. And when the bear is slain, it is in a "ceremony of innocence," to borrow Yeats' phrase: the sacred totem of the wilderness is bayed and held by the godlike dog named Lion and killed by the knife of the half-breed votary Boon Hogganbeck – the sacrificial ritual witnessed and authenticated by the high-priest Sam Fathers and the postulant Isaac McCaslin. Isaac's response to this commitment is to renounce – his land, his wealth, his public life, and even finally his marriage and the son he might have had, so that at past seventy he owns nothing but a narrow iron cot.

At witnessing once more the same defilement of the innocent that marked the establishment of his family's dynasty in this new country, he has to be reminded by a young unmarried mother (Roth's mistress) that the passion week of the heart still has efficacy: "Old man," she says, "have you lived so long and forgotten so much that you dont remember anything you ever knew or even heard about love?" (p. 212) Her rebuke recalls him to the knowledge that to love does not necessarily mean to possess – that indeed, as he learned in his youth – love is refined in the fire of denial, the anguish of desire propelling the heart into a spiritual wholeness that resembles the love of God. Isaac's life has been a hidden drama of surrender and faith.

After writing *Go Down, Moses*, a watershed in his topography, Faulkner put behind him the predominantly tragic outlook of his earlier writing and went on to the composition of works that explore the relation of renunciation to wholeness: in dark parables such as *Requiem for a Nun* and *A Fable*; in the major story of his entire imaginative life, the *Snopes Trilogy*; and, finally, in a work of affirmative power and innocent joy, *The Reivers*. The *Snopes Trilogy*, which straddles the watershed, was conceived by Faulkner in his early days as a grim tale of the triumph of evil.[4] But by the time he came to write *The Town* (1957) and *The Mansion* (1959), his vision of human life had changed, principally because of his growing awareness of the spiritual power wielded by those who sacrifice themselves, characters who make themselves "eunuchs for the kingdom of God."

In the first portion of the trilogy, *The Hamlet*, published in 1940, before *Go Down, Moses*, the center of desire is an Aphrodite figure, Eula Varner, the apparent opposite of the virgin. "Her entire appearance," we are told, "suggested some symbology out of the old Dionysic times – honey in sunlight and bursting grapes, the writhen bleeding of the crushed fecundated vine beneath the hard rapacious trampling goat-hoof."[5] She calls forth in men the desire to seize, to possess – "at once supremely chaste and inviolable: the queen, the matrix." (p. 116) She is the fecund sensual beauty, the matrix, out of which all life comes. "By merely walking down the aisle [of the schoolroom] she would transform the very wooden desks and benches themselves into a grove of Venus and fetch every male in the room, from the children just entering puberty to the grown men of nineteen and twenty...springing into embattled rivalry, importunate, each for precedence in immolation." (p. 115) Eula is the antithesis of Faulkner's unattainable Artemis figure; she is the very embodiment of fertility, the source of life careless of her power to arouse desire. And she generates an anguish akin to spiritual yearning.

In *The Town*, however, when the action of Faulkner's trilogy has moved to Jefferson and Eula, married to the impotent Flem Snopes, has long had a lover, her spiritual transformation is accomplished by the adoration and renunciation of a young lawyer, Gavin Stevens. She appears to Gavin at his office late one evening to bestow herself upon him – since the giving of her body means little to her; and Gavin's horrified recoil as from a goddess changes her life. To him she is Aphrodite Urania rather than Aphrodite Pandemos, the heavenly rather than the carnal Venus. Like Isaac McCaslin, he does not seize the object of desire when he has the chance to do so. Before this gesture of abnegation occurs, Eula has manifested the heedlessness of the feminine fertility figure; but afterwards she evidences moral reflection and sacrifice, moving towards a profound motherly concern for her daughter Linda, working with Gavin for the young woman's welfare, and finally giving her life for her daughter.

Linda, legally a Snopes though in actuality the illegitimate child of Eula and her lover of one passionate and heroic night, becomes the spiritual child of Gavin's love for Eula, his dream child, as he likes to think. She is a slim, straight young woman who, as Chick Mallison says, walks down the streets like a pointer, and as Gavin adds, "the maiden bitch of course, the virgin bitch, immune now in virginity, not scorning the earth, spurning the earth...."[6] Gavin educates her, "forms her mind," as Maggie, Gavin's twin, puts it, by lending her books, in particular the poems of John Donne, those celebrations of the metaphysical mysteries of love. After Linda has matured and found her one love, married him and lost him in the war in Spain which leaves her deafened, she returns to Jefferson and resumes her intimate friendship with her teacher Gavin Stevens. Gavin's devotion to Linda's now dead mother, Eula, enables him to share her understanding of pain and anguished love. In an almost overt reference to Keats' ode, Linda is called the "inviolate bride of silence, inviolable in maidenhead."[7] She has begun her life as the unattainable Artemis figure, but her faithful love of her lost husband transforms her into a fuller image of the virgin who, like Gavin and McCaslin, achieves completeness in dedicating her life to the transcendent purity of loving without possessing. Her virginal-motherhood overflows into the community, where she is noted for her work among the poor and dispossessed, and she shares with Gavin a relationship of erotic *philia*, a passionate friendship that contains and completes sexuality without physical consummation.

But it is Gavin's *alter ego*, V.K. Ratliff, who within himself possesses the wholeness that marks the heralding of the New Jerusalem. He has the "hearty celibacy as of a lay brother in a twelfth-century monastery—a gardener, a pruner of vines, say."[8] As Layard indicates, the monk's chief search was for love; "true celibacy...if rightly understood, [is] the most complete expression of the transformed sex instinct."[9] Faulkner's comparison is not casual, for among all the many and varied bachelors in the Snopes trilogy, Ratliff is the only one who contains a hearty and unabashed integrity, both primordial and apocalyptic, which is the sign of the New Creation. When he meets Allanova, a Russian tie designer in New York, another "virgin" who points back to Eden and forward to the fullness of eternity, they recognize each other in love and exchange an emblematic kiss of peace. But they do not "desire" each other erotically; nor do they need each other for completion. Their mutual love and recognition come from a super-abundance; they share a foretaste of the "no-giving in marriage" that is to be the blessedness of heaven.

Thus the anguished "passion week of the heart" leading to a kind of resurrection in a transformed body represents the achievement of a higher stage of love and wholeness for which the urn in its silence and beauty is symbol. This development of the highest calling of the lover in Faulkner's work is accompanied by a concomitant development in the object of desire. The feminine virginal archetype, the Kore (the Greek word for maiden), is a figure with which Faulkner was apparently preoccupied from the beginning of his writing. Each of his first two novels, *Soldier's Pay* and *Mosquitoes*, explores this image. And because they are less complex and less subtle than his later works, the articulation of an underlying mythological structure is more easily traced in them than in the masterpieces of his mature career.

Mosquitoes, Faulkner's second novel, addresses itself directly to one aspect of the archetype – the nymph or dryad. At one point in it, a young woman – Pat Robyn, usually simply referred to as the niece – hard and slim, "with the odor of young trees,"[10] is lying in her bunk on shipboard with her friend Jenny. Jenny is her antithesis, "an utterly mindless rifeness of youth, pink flesh, a supine potential fecundity lovely to look upon," (p. 85) rosy as the young dawn. The two have been comparing their differences, one concave, the other convex, and matching their fragmentary knowledge of the ways of the world, when Pat suddenly asks Jenny if she is a virgin:

> "Of course I am," Jenny answered immediately in a startled tone. She lay for a moment in lax astonishment. "I mean," she said, "I – yes. I mean, yes, of course I am." She brooded in passive surprise, then her body lost its laxness. "Say – "
>
> "Well," the niece agreed judicially. "I guess that's about what I'd have said myself." (pp. 121-22)

The two converse further, in some mistrust now as well as confidence, revealing at once their innocence as well as their innate knowledge – arising from the springs of life itself – that virginity is an ambiguous matter, both a disgrace and a virtue. These two young women, apparent opposites in a novel devoted to an examination of the relation of virginity to art, are prototypes of characters Faulkner will explore further in his succeeding novels and short stories.

On board a pleasure yacht, *Nausikaa*, named after the maiden in *The Odyssey* whom Odysseus encounters but does not possess, is an array of art lovers: a patroness of the arts, a critic, a dilettante, a novelist, and a true artist, the sculptor named Gordon. Gordon has fashioned a work of art which has a peculiar attraction for this heterogeneous crew of people. It is the torso of a young girl:

> As you entered the room the thing drew your eyes: you turned sharply as to a sound, expecting movement. But it was marble, it could not move. And when you tore your eyes away and turned your back on it at last, you got again untarnished high and clean that sense of swiftness, of space encompassed; but on looking again it was as before; motionless and passionately eternal – the virginal breastless torso of a girl, headless, armless, legless, in marble temporarily caught and hushed yet passionate still for

> escape, passionate and simple and eternal in the equivocal derisive darkness of the world. Nothing to trouble your youth or lack of it; rather something to trouble the very fibrous integrity of your being. (pp. 10-11)

"It's like me," the niece, she who is "straight as a poplar," (p. 24) says when she first views it. "I wish I could have it." But Gordon refuses to part with the statue. "This is my feminine ideal," he says brutally: "a virgin with no legs to leave me, no arms to hold me, no head to talk to me." (p.23)

Gordon too makes the connection between the niece and the sculpture. Once, when he swings her on board ship,

> for an instant she stopped in midflight, hand to hand and braced to arm, high above the deck while water dripping from her turned to gold as it fell. Sunset was in his eyes; a glory he could not see; and her taut simple body, almost breastless and with the fleeting hips of a boy, was an ecstasy in golden marble, and in her face the passionate ecstasy of a child. (p. 68)

After Pat has run away with a crew member, he broods on that "young hard graveness" of hers, which he feels about him like an odor. "No wonder she was gone out of it: she who here was as a flame among stale ashes...who gone was as a pipe blown thinly and far away...." (p. 154) Gordon, this passage makes clear, is the poet, the commentator, the observer of the Grecian Urn, who can say, with a tinge of rue: "Heard melodies are sweet, but those unheard are sweeter."

Later, conversing about art and virginity, the men agree that a man writes always for some woman – maybe not a flesh and blood woman: she may be only "the symbol of a desire." (p. 206) The niece, talking with the sculptor, discerns that he is in love with "that marble girl without any arms and legs you made." (p. 223) And Gordon, thinking to himself, meditates: "It is no pale virgin...with painted fingernails and honey and myrrh cunningly beneath her tongue.... It is dawn, in the high cold hills, dawn like a wind in the clean hills, and on the wind comes the thin piping of shepherds...." (p. 225) It is not the hetaera figure, but the divine reality embodied in the untainted Artemis, the virgin who dwells in the woods and the mountains, for which Gordon yearns.

Fairchild the novelist says to him, "you kind of wish she could talk, don't you? It would be sort of like wind through the trees...no...not talk: you'd like to watch her from a distance on a May morning, bathing in a pool where there were a lot of poplar trees." (p. 272) He has discerned the Artemis archetype in the statue, with his reference to Actaeon's viewing the goddess at her bath. Part of the anguish experienced in the yearning for Artemis stems from the fact that, as Karl Kerényi points out, her maidenhood, unlike that of Athene, is not absolute. She is attainable. "Athene's maidenhood excluded the very possibility of her succumbing to a man; with Artemis on the other hand, her maidenhood presupposes this possibility."[11] Pat Robyn, then like the figure on Keats' urn, can, in principle, be captured by a pursuing youth. Vulnerability is essential to the concept of the Kore, as apparently Faulkner discovered in pursuit of his art.

Nonetheless, the central role of abnegation in the drama of art, of forswearing the action that desire demands, would persist throughout the lengthy canon of Faulkner's work. In this early novel *Mosquitoes*, it is the novelist Fairchild who, later that evening, "listening to the dark and measured beating of things," enunciates what Gordon really knows about his art and what the others have been confusedly discussing:

> "That's what it is, Genius.... People confuse it so, you see. They have got it now to where it signifies only an active state of mind in which a picture is painted or a poem is written. When it is not that at all. It is that Passion Week of the heart, that instant of timeless beatitude which some never know, which some, I suppose, gain at will, which others gain through an outside agency like alcohol — that passive state of the heart with which the mind, the brain, has nothing to do at all, in which the hackneyed accidents which make up this world — love and life and death and sex and sorrow — brought together by chance in perfect proportions, take on a kind of splendid and timeless beauty." (p. 339)

It is important to note that this "instant of timeless beatitude" is described as a "passive state of the heart with which the mind, the brain, has nothing to do at all." Surrender, submission to the real, self-abandonment — what Keats calls "negative capability" — is the requisite condition for this "passion week of the heart" in which the "accidents" of life take on a "splendid and timeless beauty."

Mosquitoes is openly concerned with the lover's virginity — that state of yearning and yet renouncing, in which as Walter Otto has said, the human mind becomes creative by being "touched and inspired by a wonderful Otherness."[12] Yet it treats most fully of the image of desire: that of the seemingly inviolable ideal.

Faulkner establishes in this early novel the connection of the nymph, or dryad, with water and with trees. One is able to understand more clearly from this early novel why Candace Compson, in the later work *The Sound and the Fury*, smells, to her idiot brother Benjy, "like trees," and why, when she is corrupted by a loveless promiscuity, he howls inconsolably at the loss of her clean fresh aura of vegetation. *Mosquitoes* also establishes the poles of the maiden figure – the two young women, so unlike at first glance, Jenny and Robyn, are parts of the same whole: the fertility figure and the virginal figure are both aspects of the Kore, the maiden. Faulkner had earlier depicted the union of this configuration in the person of Margaret Powers of *Soldier's Pay*, one of the young women centered around the wounded soldier, Donald Mahon, who has come home to die.

Mrs. Powers is a type of Ariadne. As Otto has said, "Ariadne is maiden and nurse, or mother, at one and the same time, like Artemis, and the dreadful shadows of death play about her figure as they do about that of the goddess.... Theseus, the son of Poseidon, abducts her. Dionysus, who disappears into the watery depths and emerges from them again, becomes her bridegroom."[13] *Soldier's Pay*, at least on one level, is a story of the dying Dionysus; in a world in which the institutional church is losing its efficacy, Dionysus must make his perennial sacrifice. He is, as Otto reminds us, "the child of a mortal mother, and just as he must endure suffering and death, so the women with whom he is most intimately associated reach a state of glory only by passing through deep sorrow."[14]

Soldier's Pay is a kind of parable of the decline of the West – its loss of an adequate religion, its loosening of morality, its psychic disillusion. The novel is, as has been pointed out, Faulkner's *Waste Land*; and, as in Eliot's work, the Christianity that pervades this vision of a dying culture finds expression in the survivors, characters who will endure and prevail. For Margaret Powers and Joe Gilligan are moved by more than secular meliorism in their acts of generosity; it is *caritas* that governs these guardians, and *Soldier's Pay* ends with their growing hope and still distant possibility of faith. They move in a pagan world, however, and pagan gods participate. The most obviously identifiable is Pan, the orphan god, of late comings and sudden epiphanies.[15] The character named Januarius Jones, "born of whom he knew and cared not,"[16] appears in the garden of the Episcopalian rector of lost belief. The rector greets him "against an ivy-colored wall above which the consummate grace of a spire and a gilded cross seemed to arc across motionless young clouds." (p. 40) Observing the spire's "illusion of slow ruin," Jones comments to the rector, "Watch it fall, sir." Jones is described as a satyr, as yellow-eyed, goatlike. He "knows panic" and arouses panic in others; around him whirls a mild pandemonium.

He views Cecily Saunders, Donald Mahon's fiancee, as a hamadryad, "epicene." She is slim as a young tree; her voice is "like a tangle of golden wires": "He could imagine her long subtle legs, like Atalanta's reft of running." (p. 55) Cecily, however, is terrified of Jones; she feels her young clearness to be like water; she is utterly self-centered and self-contained. It becomes increasingly apparent to Margaret Powers and to Jones that Cecily will not go through with her marriage to the injured soldier, even to give him some chance at recovery. Jones, however, continues his pursuit of her, a "fat Mirandola in a chaste Platonic nympholepsy, a religious-sentimental orgy in gray tweed, shaping an insincere, fleeting articulation of damp clay to an old imperishable desire, building himself a papier maché Virgin." (p. 156) "Dammit, do you think all a man wants of you is your body?" (p. 157) he asks once in exasperation. But if he wishes only to revel in his nympholepsy—his ecstatic worship of a nymph — with Cecily, he chases another young woman, Emmy, as sexual object and apparently satisfies his lust upon her.

Emmy, the third of the attendant "nurses," a shy, sheltered daughter of a harsh father, has had one experience of love in her life: Donald Mahon courted her, despite her father's disapproval. One evening, or so she recounts the story to a sympathetic Mrs. Powers, Donald came for her and they went swimming together in the moonlight.

> "I could see him running along the top of the hill, all shiny in the moonlight, then he ran back down the hill toward the creek. And so I laid down, I couldn't see anything except the sky, and I don't know how long it was when all of a sudden there was his head against the sky, over me, and he was wet again, and I could see the moonlight kind of running on his wet shoulders and arms, and he

> looked at me. I couldn't see his eyes, but I could feel them somehow like things touching me. When he looks at you—you feel like a bird, kind of: like you was going swooping right away from the ground or something." (pp. 88-89)

Emmy expresses here the ecstasy of the Dionysian experience, to which she will remain faithful. As Otto points out, "The Bacchant pays no attention to the silenus who grabs at her in his lust; the image of Dionysus whom she loves, stands alive before her soul and she sees him even though he is far away from her...."[17]

It is Mrs. Powers, of the three "virgins" who nurse Donald Mahon, who comes to an understanding of what love is. Her own marriage had been hasty, precipitated beyond betrothal by the necessity of her soldier's leaving for the front. In quest of meaning for her life, she shares with Joe Gilligan – a soldier who has also come to the aid of Donald Mahon – her concern for the injured soldier and for Cecily's desertion of him, hence her marriage to Mahon in order to brighten the last remaining week of his life. After Mahon's death, she is certain, though she herself begins to return Joe's affection, that they are not meant to marry nor to consummate their love. The two have given themselves without stint to the care of the wounded soldier; and now, she tells him, they must go their separate ways in the world.

Mahon, re-enacting the passion of Dionysus-Christ, the eternally suffering god, is surrounded by three women, three nurses of a sort: the nymph Cecily; Emmy the "dishonored virgin" (p. 49) as Januarius Jones calls her, whom Mahon has once taken as his beloved; and Margaret Powers, widow of a sailor killed in the war, who becomes Mahon's bride and endures his suffering with him. Otto informs us that the young women surrounding Dionysus are "maidens of moisture," and they become his nurses. "There are almost always three sisters with whom the god comes into contact,"[18] he says, and we meet "this circle of sisters again and again."[19] The figure of Pan in the character of Jones seems to symbolize the recurrence of that indestructible and unruly life force that emerges – even though the Great God Pan was declared dead – whenever a society is in danger of turning away from the mysteries of life.

Faulkner's first two novels show us an intertwining of several of his imaginative figures, depicted more fully and more subtly in his later work. The unselfish and unconsummated love between Margaret and Joe Gilligan pre-figures that of Linda Snopes and Gavin

Stevens, as well as Ratliff and Allanova. Januarius Jones, as Pan, is a comic portrayal of the artist who wants to contemplate, without violating, his nymph and who ends by animalistically seizing another woman. Gordon, the sculptor, is a more serious portrayal of the artist who out of devotion to his ideal, like Isaac McCaslin in the later work, undergoes the passion of immolation. The two sides of the Kore figure are depicted in Pat and Jenny, Cecily and Emmy, coming together in Margaret Powers. Faulkner will sound the variations on these themes, moving toward their reconciliation and harmony in his later writing.

The Kore figure, as the potentially attainable ideal, emerges more fully in the character of Lena Grove, both mother and maiden, in *Light in August*. She has commonly been called a type of earth mother, since she carries within her the child who will bring life back to the town of Jefferson and to its minister, Gail Hightower. Hightower can foresee her peopling the good earth with her kind. Yet Faulkner likens her to a figure on an urn and to the slow movement of the seasons, her name is Grove, and she maintains the self-possession of a Kore figure. She is simply, as Faulkner tells us, looking for a father for her child, without anxiety. Unashamed, she moves with great dignity, though in the last stage of pregnancy, into a town which has a strict taboo against her particular violation of the code. But Byron Bunch falls in love with her irrevocably at first sight, as one does with one of the hard-to-attain maidens in mythology; he undergoes difficulties to win her—and indeed, even by the end of the novel has not yet secured that end, though she has indicated that she returns his love. Lena requires of her suitor courtship, though she has never had that consideration before. She is essentially virginal, even if she does bear with her on her journeyings the evidence of her maternity. Faulkner gives Lena the vitality and assurance of being in herself complete, as though the father of her child has been Zeus himself.[20]

The Grecian urn image which I have been exploring has been frequently interpreted by Faulkner commentators as representing a temptation to a platonic stasis, ideal and beautiful but far removed from life, implying, indeed, a rejection of life because of mortal imperfection.[21] Instead, as I am arguing, the image is for Faulkner one of intense vitality, inclusive of the whole of "motion," consecrated, holy, alive. The source of this intense vitality, as I think we can see, is love. The heart must be virginal if it is to love; and what it loves is endowed with an unending virginal freshness. Faulkner's dedicated characters, through renouncing, love more keenly and deeply, more spiritually and fully. Their dedication is symbolized in Faulkner's novels by celibacy: Margaret Powers and Joe Gilligan, Judith Sutpen, the later Gail Hightower, Isaac McCaslin, the early Gavin Stevens, Linda Snopes, V.K. Ratliff.

But if the human enterprise is to endure and prevail on earth, the new life must at least at times come through consummation. Thus in the comic vision the lover must be able to attain the maiden: she must combine the slim "epicene" purity with a fleshly and quite earthly reality. The two opposites in Jenny and Pat, Eula and Linda come together in Lena and, above all, in Corrie.

The culmination of the Kore figure – mother and maiden – is to be found in the prostitute of Faulkner's last novel, *The Reivers*, Everbe Corinthia, called Corrie. Corinth is the place, of course, where Paul visited to preach by necessity the crucified Christ, and to speak, by permission, of virginity; the subject was appropriate for the site because Corinth was famous for its prostitutes – so much so that, until recent years, the phrase "to go to Corinth" meant to visit a brothel. Though there were many independent professionals in the city, the chief attraction was the temple dedicated to Aphrodite, served by a thousand priestesses or sacred prostitutes. Not only did they bring affluence to their city but they also interceded with their goddess for the benefit of Corinthians. When the city was in peril from the Persians under Xerxes, it was the prayers of the prostitutes that were credited with turning the enemy away.[22]

The name Corinthia is also of course associated with the epistles to the Corinthians wherein St. Paul delineates that *caritas* without which a person is "nothing." Love suffers, seeks not her own, bears all things, believes all things, hopes all things, endures all things. This figure of that which is essentially supernatural, a gift to man, has been portrayed by Dante as Beatrice, by Shakespeare as Cordelia and Imogen, by Dostoevsky as Sonia. For Faulkner, Everbe Corinthia, incorruptible, truthful, loving, symbolizes the divine love which, entering the mortal realm, suffers degradation. She is that *caritas* of which man is constantly in quest, a love which is ever self-immolating and ever pure – eternally virgin. The heroine of *The Reivers*, then, bears a fitting and undoubtedly deliberately chosen name.[23] The shortened form of it – Corrie – is a homonym for the Greek word for *maiden* which we have been using: Kore. And as for Corrie's other name — Everbe — it seems calculated to evoke the poem that could be called the controlling image for Faulkner's work, Keats' "Ode on a Grecian Urn." Young Lucius Priest finds in Corrie (who reveals to him that her real name is Everbe) his image of the beautiful virgin: "Forever wilt thou love and she be fair." Thus it is the innocence of a boy — and of a boy who has "fallen" by helping Boon Hogganbeck steal Lucius' Grandfather's car for a trip to Memphis — that evokes in Everbe Corinthia her true nature.

As Layard reminds us, the word *virgin* in all the ancient languages — Hebrew, Greek, Latin — means not *chaste*, but unmarried, unpossessed.[24a] It is a legal, not a natural, distinction. It hence expresses the value of the feminine person in herself, apart from her relation to a man. The virgin belongs to herself, at least in the temporal order. Layard tells us that "The prostitute is the archetype of the free woman, the woman untrammeled by man's laws."[24b] Hence, though her situation is deplorable and though she is certainly not socially respectable, something powerfully feminine has been preserved in Everbe, something which the boy recognizes and honors. She makes a pledge to him to give up her way of life — to the dismay of Boon Hogganbeck (who has saved his money for this trip to the Memphis whorehouse: "Why now?" he asks in desperation). Boon finds, to his consternation, that in order to possess Corrie, he will have to marry her, though to his credit it must be said that he does in fact fall in love with her. The story ends happily with their marriage, and, in due time, the birth of a child.

Magdalene figure, maiden, Venus, and madonna — these are the apparently contradictory typologies contained in this masterful portrayal of the fulfillment of the Kore figure in *The Reivers*. As Kerényi has written, "The Kore-goddess throws light on the old mythological idea in its bud-like capacity to unfold and yet to contain a whole compact world in itself. The idea can also be likened to a nucleus. We have to understand as it were the structure hidden in the abyss of the nucleus."[25]

The structure hidden in the abyss of the nucleus of the Kore-goddess is nothing short of the "eternal woman" of whom Gertrud von le Fort writes: "Thus from dogma, history, saga, and art, the idea of virginity emerges, not as a transitory condition or a tragedy, but as a value and a power."[26] It is the completion of himself for which man yearns, Faulkner indicates; yet paradoxically the satisfaction of the yearning leaves him unsatisfied. Nothing short of the eternally desirable can be equal to his passion, to what Gavin Stevens calls "that chewed anguish of the poet's bitter thumbs."[27]

The outcroppings of myth in the writings of great artists are frequent and undeniable, providing, as it were, a subterranean current of communication between author and reader whereby large aggregates of affective awareness are called forth. The myths, in the West, primarily those of Greek and Hebraic origins mingled with Christianity, have so shaped language and response that even when unrecognized in a particular instance, they set up their characteristic resonances. And yet it is not so much that the artist seeks to use the myth to accomplish his ends as that he intends to acknowledge that what has come to him as an epiphany, directly out of the region of archetypes, has elsewhere made its appearances and is indeed immanent.

For Faulkner, the archetype of the virgin appeared early in his career, beckoning him toward his appointed path, providing the function if not the form of a Beatrice. Lover, beloved, mentor, wilderness, mother, sister, goddess, prostitute, poet, guardian—all of these avatars manifest in Faulkner's works the virginal quality that transcends sexuality and that, fully realized, is taken out of time and placed in the temple of the eternal as these images assume their places on the all-containing urn that is the totality of Faulkner's achievement.

1. William Faulkner, *Go Down, Moses* (New York: Random House, Modern Library edition, 1942), pp. 296-97. All further citations from this edition will be indicated by page numbers in the text.
2. John Layard, "The Incest Taboo and the Virgin Archetype" (see pp. 145-184, this book).
3. Faulkner, *Mosquitoes* (New York: Dell Publishing Co., Inc., 1965), p. 280.
4. For a summary of the original story see Joseph Blotner, *Faulkner: A Biography* (New York: Random House, 1974), pp. 1006-8. Eileen Gregory's "The Temerity to Revolt: Mink Snopes and the Dispossessed in *The Mansion*," *Mississippi Quarterly* XXIX, 3 (Summer, 1976) provides a fine analysis of the ominousness of Snopesism and Faulkner's gradual change in attitude toward it.
5. Faulkner, *The Hamlet* (New York: Random House, Vintage Books, 1959), p. 95.
6. Faulkner, *The Town* (New York: Random House, Vintage Books, 1957), p. 132.
7. Faulkner, *The Mansion* (New York: Random House, Vintage Books, 1959), p. 203.
8. Faulkner, *The Hamlet*, p. 43.
9. Layard, p. 167. This and all further citations refer to the present volume.
10. Faulkner, *Mosquitoes*, p. 19.

11. Karl Kerényi, "Kore," in C.G. Jung and Karl Kerényi, *Essays on A Science of Mythology* (Princeton, N.J.: Princeton University Press, 1971), p. 107.

12. Walter F. Otto, *Dionysus: Myth and Cult* (Bloomington and London: Indiana University Press, 1965), p. 21, reprinted by Spring Publications, Dallas, Texas, 1981.

13. Otto, p. 184.

14. Otto, p. 185.

15. See James Hillman, *An Essay on Pan,* in W.H. Roscher and Hillman, *Pan and the Nightmare* (Zürich: Spring Publications, 1972).

16. Faulkner, *Soldier's Pay* (New York/Toronto: New American Library, Signet Modern Classic, 1968), p. 40.

17. Otto, p. 177.

18. Otto, p. 172.

19. Otto, p. 173.

20. See Faulkner's comment on Lena in *Faulkner in the University*, Frederick L. Gwynn and Joseph L. Blotner, eds. (New York: Vintage Books, 1965), p. 199.

21. For discussion of Faulkner's use of the Grecian urn ode see Darrel Abel, "Frozen Moment in *Light in August,*" *Boston University Studies in English,* III (Spring, 1957), p. 33; Michael Millgate, *The Achievement of William Faulkner* (New York: Random House, 1966); Richard P. Adams, *Faulkner: Myth and Motion* (Princeton: Princeton University Press, 1968); J.F. Kobler, "Lena Grove: Faulkner's Still Unravished Bride of Quietness," *Arizona Quarterly,* XXVIII (Winter, 1972), pp. 340-41; and Joan S. Korenman, "Faulkner's Grecian Urn," *The Southern Literary Journal,* VII (Fall, 1974), pp. 3-20.

22. Robert Flaceliere, *Love in Ancient Greece*, tr. James Cluegh (New York: Crown Publishers, 1962), p. 135.

23. Faulkner used her name once before, at the very beginning of his career, in a grotesque tale, "The Leg," written in 1925 and published in *Dr. Martino and Other Stories* (New York: Smith and Haas, 1934). In this story she likewise represents innocent love and purity which is violated tragically by a cruel and demonic man. It is as though Faulkner carried her name and image with him throughout his life and was able to save her for human culture only at the end of his career.

24a. Layard, p. 170. 24b. Layard, p. 178.

25. Kerényi, p. 106.

26. Gertrud von le Fort, *The Eternal Woman* (Milwaukee: The Bruce Publishing Co., 1962), p. 25.

27. Faulkner, *The Town,* p. 90.

Womb of Gold, Body of the Sun Reflections on Christian Imagery of the Virgin and the Moon

David L. Miller

> Lord, have mercy on my son who is moonstruck.... For he falls often into the fire and often into the water.
>
> —Matthew 17.15

Kyrie eleison! The New Testament's miracle-story of the healing of the so-called "epileptic" boy opens with these words which have become well-known through centuries of liturgical use and through lifetimes of hurt. "Lord, have mercy." The petition refers, in this case, to a particular disease. Modern translators commonly refer to it as "epilepsy," but the Greek word in the Bible carries a more imaginal name. *Seleniadzetai* literally means "moonstruck,"[1] and the boy's father explains this problem enigmatically by telling Jesus that his son falls into the fire and into water.

The healing-narrative continues by revealing that the disciples have been therapeutic failures in regard to the boy's difficulty. The father says, "I brought him to your disciples, but they could not heal him (*ouk...therapeusai*)." These words make Jesus angry. His response is strong. Why—he asks rhetorically—does he have to put up with a generation that is so "perverse" and of such "little faith" (*oligopistian*). Then Jesus himself turns to the boy and speaks to the "soul" of the disease (*to daimonion*). At this, as the Bible says, "the boy is healed immediately."[2]

Why were the disciples not able to be therapeutic in this case? Were they not able to handle real "lunacy"?[3] The text implies that their inability had something to do with "little faith." But what is meant by this phrase (*oligopistian*), and in what way is it a clue to therapeutic failure?

There is some immediate *theological* awkwardness even in raising these questions. Orthodox traditions of Judaism and Christianity have been reticent to make too much of the Moon, as if they themselves have "little faith" with regard to this night-light. In Deuteronomy, for example, there is a typical prohibition: "Thou shalt not lift up thine eyes unto heaven and see the Sun, Moon, and Stars...and be led astray to worship and serve them."[4] Also, about Christians, Celsus observes that they "reject...the Sun and Moon...they think them of no account."[5]

However, the tradition is by no means completely ambivalent. Origen, for example, responds to Celsus on behalf of the Church, saying that its perspective is *not*, as Celsus thinks, like that of Anaxagoras, who views the planets to be "mere lumps of hot metal." Rather, Origen says, the Sun, Moon, and Stars are "heralds of God, heavenly messengers."[6] Similarly, Alexander Neckam, in the twelfth century, calls the Moon a gift of the Holy Spirit because it brings *timoris dei*, a proper "fear of God."[7] Saint Ambrose is even more enthusiastic when he says: "Truly blessed art thou, Luna, who hast been found worthy of such honor. For Luna hath declared unto us the mystery of Christ."[8] Theophilus of Antioch agrees: "These lights, the Sun and Moon, enact and show forth a great mystery."[9]

So, in spite of the prohibition against imagining the Moon ultimately to have power over life, there is nonetheless an acknowledgment in orthodox Western theology of what one writer has called the *mysterium lunae*.[10] An inquiry into this "moon mystery" may provide some insight with regard to the miracle-story of a "moonstruck" boy whom Jesus healed and over whom Jesus' followers seemed to have no therapeutic ability.

Mysterium Lunae: Testimonia Theologica

The Church's official theology of Moon-symbolism is clear and straightforward. Mary is the Moon. Like the planet which circles us, she *reflects* the light of the Sun, who is Christ. It is in this way that we can have divine light in our world. We would not be able to take it in direct doses. It is too hot and too bright. So, it is mediated by the cooler and softer manner of the Woman. By contemplating this mediation, particularly, and the relationship between the Sun and the Moon, generally, we can come to understand the mystery of Christ. Thus, the planets bring a divine message, being reflections of the holy Gospel.

The Church's tradition of piety concerning this lunar symbolism has waxed poetic, as the following examples will demonstrate. The first is from Peter Chrysologus who wrote in the fifth century.

> Having passed through its appointed annual course, the day of the Lord's nativity arrives and the splendor of the virgin birth is spread in fiery brilliance over the whole earth.[11]

This sentence trades on a metaphor used by the prophet, Malachi: "The Sun shall rise with healing in its wings."[12] The Church interprets this Messianic prophecy to refer to Jesus, as can be seen in the words written over a pre-gothic miniature of the Virgin:

> In the womb of the Mother lives the Wisdom of the Father.
> The Moon caresses the Sun from whom she herself derived the light.[13]

Compare this with the following hymn of fourteenth-century French flagellants:

> Ave Regina, pure and loving,
> Most noble; Ave maris stella,
> Ave, dear Maid,
> Moon where God took hiding.
> But for the Virgin Mary
> The world would have been lost.[14]

There is also this from a thirteenth-century Latin hymn:

> From Luna shines the glow of the Sun, God's ray,
> Her steadfast motions show to men His way.
> When Sun and Moon unite, darkness flies away,
> And all things grow more bright.[15]

The physical and somewhat erotic idea of God "hiding" in Mary's womb, as the Sun "hides" in the Moon during a New Moon or during an Eclipse, together with the notion of the Sun and Moon "uniting," is made more explicit in the lines of Anastasius:

> Oh, never again vanish into the darkness of the renewing Moon,
> Ever-shining Selene.
> Lighten our way through the divinely hidden meaning
> Of the Scriptures.
> Oh, cease not,
> Thou consort and fellow-traveller of Christ, the Sun,
> Who, as thy Bridegroom, clothes thee with light.
> Oh, cease not
> To send forth thy rays which from Him have taken their brightness,
> So that out of Himself, but through Thee,
> He may give light to the stars,
> And set them on fire,
> Through thee for thyself.[16]

There is here an allusion to an image in the Book of Revelation: "A great portent appeared in heaven, a woman clothed with the Sun, with the Moon under her feet."[17] This same Biblical image is continued in Carolingian and Early Medieval painting which typically shows Mary standing on the Moon, clearly pregnant, with an aura of rays emitting, not from her head in halo-fashion, but from around her full womb.[18]

The poetry of the Church not only celebrates the fact that Mary, like the Moon, gives forth Divine Fire. It also pictures her, like the Moon and like the Church, as granting life-giving moisture. So Macrobius, in late Roman times, writes:

> There is in Moon's light something that flows down from it and soaks everything with a hidden dew.[19]

John Lydos and Methodius of Philippi are even more direct about this.

> Selene (as mistress over all waters and humours and as thus the vital principle of life) is the primal cause of all birth.[20]

> The Church stands upon the Moon. By Selene, in my view, the Scripture seeks to indicate, by means of an image, the faith of

> those who have been cleansed by the power of baptism. For the light of Selene has a kind of relationship to water, and all things that are of moist substance are dependent upon Selene.[21]

So Mary is viewed as *humorum mater*.[22] In her there is and through her there comes both fire and water.[23] These apparently opposite elements and qualities are one in the image of the Virgin.

The lunar poetry of Christian piety is unambiguously forthright about the Moon, even if orthodox theology is cautious. The hymns of the people seem as "moonstruck" as the diseased boy to whose *daimon* Jesus spoke.

But perhaps the Church Fathers were right to be reticent. Lurking at the edges of this poetic theology is an implicit craziness. One begins to see the lunacy of the lovely lunar poetry as the pagan background of Moon-Sun imagery is uncovered.

Lunatic Perversity in Pagan Myth

Already in the Christian images of Mary-as-Moon and Christ-as-Sun there are implicit problems of jumbled family relationships. The Moon is viewed as Mother to a Son who is himself the source of the very fire which impregnates his Mother. This makes Christ the Father of himself and, at the same time, Son of himself. Is this what is intended? It would be an imagining of a Child who is the very one who fathers, and of a Father as one who is Child of himself in himself, as if one person carries both Parent and Progeny and as if each of these is known only in relation to the other.

There is another problem. Anastasius' word, "bridegroom," hints at incest. Mary, or so the images suggest, is wed to her own Son. This not only carries an erotic undertone; it also implies that sons are sometimes wed to whatever mothers them, and that mothers are mated to whatever they bear. It is as if whatever Mothers wed becomes a Child to them, and whatever one weds as a Child mothers one. Freud had a psychological name for such fantasies. He called them "polymorphous perversity."

If "perversity" is implicit in the poetry of Christian piety, it becomes overt in pagan myths which the Church borrowed and subsequently "baptized" for purposes of preaching. For example, a pertinent saying by Parmenides hints at seduction on the part of the Moon: "Selene ever looks shyly toward the penetrating rays of Helios."[24] Zeno of Verona turns this hint into a story.

> Even Luna shows in herself all the characteristics of humanity. She first appears as a scarcely visible crescent. It is as if she were a child of tender years, just come from the cradle. Then she grows slowly into a girl and then into a damsel, and as she follows her wide course and fulfills her task in the world, she daily grows older. When she is finally grown, and the golden fire of the flaming, light-giving charioteer has caused the small circle of her silver disc to become fully rounded—her own travail having been not less than that of her brother—then she inclines slowly toward old age, until having been wholly consumed by death, she starts her life a-fresh. And so, as the fiery seed of her life breaks again and again into flame, she unites the end of that life with the beginning.[25]

In this narrative, Zeno adds a dimension of meaning that is not explicit in Christian reflection on the Moon-as-Mother: namely, the Moon as sister to the Sun who is her brother. This implies that husband and wife, and son and mother, are additionally and simultaneously brother and sister. Boethius expressed this when he said: "Now, when she is full and encounters all her brother's rays / The Moon causes all lesser stars to disappear."[26] Similarly, Firmicus Maternus, before he converted to Christianity, asserted brother/sister incest in terms of Sun and Moon.

> She dims the rays of her light as it were out of respect for Sol, in the hope that once again graced with her brother's fires...reborn and renewed, she may go her way clad in radiant splendor and light.... O Luna, thou art set in the remotest region of heaven and art ever remade with thy monthly waxing light to ensure the permanence of the seeds of life. Shine thou with the royal rays of Sol.[27]

Mythic backgrounds to Christian imagery such as these imply the following incest-fantasy: the one I may have thought was wife is also mother and sister to me, just as the sister mothers me, and the mother is that one to which I may well be wed, *etc.* Husband is brother is son who husbands like a brother, *etc.* Such incest-fantasies are like the round-dance of the planets. As Plutarch put it:

> Selene is the mistress of all earthly life, for she, in her love for Helios, continually circles round him, and by union with him she receives the power to give birth.[28]

Just how radical this really is becomes perhaps clearer by noting the multiple meanings implicit in the language of a Christmas hymn written by Saint Ambrose. His liturgical poem is meant to be a Latin version of Psalm 19:4b-6, which reads:

> In them he has set a tent for the Sun,
> Which comes forth like a bridegroom leaving his chamber,
> And like a giant, runs its course with joy.
> Its rising is from the end of the heavens,
> And its circuit to the end of them;
> And there is nothing hid from its heat.

Ambrose's version reads:

> *Procedat e thalamo suo*
> *Pudoris aula regia*
> *Geminae gigas substantiae*
> *Alacris ut currat viam.*[29]

The usual translation is:

> He proceeds out of his bridal chamber,
> A royal court of chastity (or modesty),
> This giant of two substances,
> Cheerful to run his course.

There is nothing "wrong" with this translation. But more is happening in the autonomous meaning of the imagery of Ambrose's words, a "more" which might be missed without a knowledge of the pagan backgrounds that have been cited. Particularly, the terms, *thalamo*, *pudoris*, and *aula*, have deeper significance than the translation shows. *Thalamo*, indeed, means "bridal chamber"; but it also denotes specifically the "bed" or "the secret inner room [of the bride's body]." *Pudoris*, like its English cognate, "pudendum," means "sexuality," "genitalia," or, as Ovid used it,[30] "red skin." "Royal court" is a possible translation of *aula regia*, and it was surely what the Christian theologian intended. But the term, *aula*, apart from an author's rhetorical will, means the "inner room," which is to say, a particular court: the inner place of the bride's red sexuality.

One could miss the carnal connotations in the Christian hymn if one were to assume only the spirituality of the Hebrew Psalm as background. But the images of pagan mythology can reawaken connections between soul and body which the Church's piety might obscure by its reticence concerning the full significance of the Moon. In a mythic context, Ambrose's Hymn carries in its rich language the following connotations:

> Christ proceeds out of her body's bridal chamber, which is a regal room, Mary's blushing genitalia. This giant (like Selene, the Moon, herself a Titan) has two natures (Fire and Water): He is happy in such a round-dance!

To be sure, two important and traditional theological ideas are vulnerable to such a reading. This may be why the Church was hesitant about a full lunar theology while the poetry of the people was bold.

First, there is the heretical notion that Mary, rather than God the Father, is the source of Christ. The Sun, in this mythology, comes out of the Moon, rather than being that which is reflected by the Moon. The Female is the source of the Male, rather than being the cool reflection of his brilliance. Salvation is from the Virgin.

Second, and perhaps just as embarrassing to certain versions of doctrine and belief, is the matter of Mary's eroticism. The idea of the virginity of the Virgin is at stake. However, the terms for "virgin" in Hebrew (*'almah*), Greek (*parthenos*), and Latin (*virgo*) are already ambiguous. It has often been pointed out that they can mean something other than biological chastity.[31] A more pristine sense of these words is like the modern use of the term in the phrase "virgin forest." The meaning has to do with being untouched by civilization and its ways, that is, with bulldozers and roads, cities and cement. So, the old words which we now render by our term "virgin" can mean "untouched," not by the male body, but by social contracts of marriage. The Hebrew, Greek, and Latin words can signify simply "unwed," without regard to sexual status. After all, the lush density and full beauty of a "virgin forest" suggest already a good deal of profligacy, not unlike the erotic, physical beauty of the Moon's round-dance with the Sun. The imagery seems to imply something deeper than social behavior.

Perhaps this deeper matter is contained subtly in the genealogy at the beginning of the book of Matthew.[32] In the chronicle of generations from David to Jesus, there is an interesting lack of reference to women. One might have expected that if so few women are to be named in this important genealogy, they would certainly be righteous figures. But the fact is that they are all noted prostitutes! (1) Tamar, disguised as a whore, seduced her father-in-law. (2) Rahab is surely the most infamous professional harlot in Scripture. (3) Ruth seduced her husband's kinsman, Boaz. (4) Bathsheba's exploits are well-known.

The verse which follows this strange list says:

> Now the birth of Jesus Christ took place in this way. When his mother Mary had been betrothed to Joseph, *before they came together* she was found to be with child....[33]

The writer of this Gospel then concludes the section by saying: "All this took place to fulfill what the Lord had spoken by the prophet: 'Behold, a *parthenos* shall conceive and bear a son....' "[34]

Was this author saying simply that an "unwed woman" was the source of a Savior? Was he indicating that Mary was, in this respect, like Tamar, Rahab, Ruth, and Bathsheba – that is, that she was *so* fruitful that she could be a prodigal source of a Light which hides in her Eros? This would imply that the astonishing miracle of the Virgin Birth has little to do with female biology or moral behavior, but that it attests to the wonderful fact that something deep and sacred hides in and can emerge from everyday life, something even that may not conform to secular social sanctions. Or perhaps the implication is that one can be "pregnant" in non-literal ways (by a Ghost! by something that "haunts" or "spirits"), and that such "pregnancy" of soul's body bears real fruit in literal history, in the flesh of everyday life. Such possibilities bear reflection.

Moonshine, Fire-Water, and Soul

Reflection might focus on theological doctrine and belief (the virginity of the Virgin, the figure of Mary as reflecting the light of Christ, *etc.*). Or, it might concentrate on meanings in the personal, social realm (the ethics of sexual behavior, *imitatio christi, etc.*). But, as we have already seen, the *images* of traditional religion, when deepened by reference to pagan mythic background (Mary-the-Moon as sister-wife-mother of Christ-the-Sun), do not lend themselves easily to doctrinal theology or to moral prescription. Serious theology is surely more than romantic, fairy-tale fictions about stars dancing! And how can a sister behaviorally be wife to her own brother? Are we to behave like Rahab and call it morality?

In the realm of doctrine and literal history, such suggestions are absurd. They make no sense.

Yet the images of religion, for whatever social and theological significance they may indirectly carry, also "mean" something in a different realm of human experience. As Jung was often to remind us,[35] the images of religion are in fact a psychology, an articulate *logos* of the self's meaning. Nor is this view concerning the *nature* of the sense of religion's imagery totally foreign to theological thinking. Ambrose and Origen both gave clue, indeed they gave sanction, to a way of viewing Christian images as referring to soul. The former wrote: "Watch the Moon, not only with fleshly eye, but with the living power of the spirit."[36] Origen was even more psychologically explicit: "Understand that you are a second little world, and that the Sun and Moon are within you."[37] In this perspective, the erotic round-dance of Mary and Jesus is "within" each of us. The lunar religious imagery is an expression of archetypal aspects of self. Theology, in this way, makes psychology, but only if the theology is read mythopoetically rather than socially or doctrinally.

Just how theology is formative for a sense of self is especially noteworthy in the case of Mary-as-Moon and Christ-as-Sun. Since Christ is viewed as divine and Mary is seen as human, the image of the former can be understood as corresponding psychologically to transpersonal and autonomous factors of the deep self (the gold of the Sun), whereas the image of the latter would then correspond to the historical ego (the silver Moon). Thus, an *orthodox* Christian psychology would view the function of the ego (1) to "integrate" dimensions of self, as Moon becomes pregnant with Sun, (2) to remain behaviorally chaste by not "acting out" the complexes, as Mary is, in orthodox perspective, virginal, and (3) to "reflect" the deep self without becoming confused with it, like the advice of *imitatio christi*. In this way an *orthodox* Christian theology of Sun and Moon gives shape and content to a psychology of individuation where there is thought to be a clearly differentiated ego-self axis. This is reminiscent of Jung's writings in Volumes VII and IX of the *Collected Works*, especially the early essays, "On the Psychology of the Unconscious" and "The Relations between the Ego and the Unconscious." These psychological works have a structure that is suspiciously similar to the traditional "supernaturalism" of Saint Thomas Aquinas and to the "infinite qualitative distinction between divine and human" of Søren Kierkegaard.

But at other places in the *Collected Works*, Jung labored to make distinctions between the orthodox perspectives of Christian psychology and, say, the more radical views of alchemy.[38] Orthodox theological perspectives, he went so far as to say, make bad psychology.[39] The reason is, as he showed, that distinguishing too much between divine and human (self and ego) has a way of unrealistically splitting what archetypally belongs together. Often, one side of an image is devalued while the other is inflated. This sort of judgment is unpsychological and repressive.

For example, Jung insisted that the Christian notion of evil as *privatio boni* is "responsible for a too optimistic conception of the evil in human nature and for a too pessimistic view of the human soul."[40] So he "corrected" the doctrine psychologically, amplifying it with heretical mythology from Gnostic sources. Jung did similar things in the cases of baptism, the Mass, and Christology, using material from astrology, alchemy, mythology, and oriental philosophy.[41]

This essay is attempting something of the sort with respect to the Church's Moon-theology. When pagan myth is allowed to amplify the Church's piety, psychological perspectives become fuller and more complete.

For example, Mary and Christ can no longer be viewed as symbolizing ego and self. Rather, both are imaginal figures of a divine drama, a round-dance which has erotic, incestuous, carnal, and mythic dimensions. Sun and Moon (Christ and Mary) are two aspects of the self, two sides of an archetypal configuration. Neither is to be integrated into the other. Both are dancing and loving. How could one think either pole of this complex to be chaste. Their mutual interpenetration is profligate and contaminating. Mary's Moon is not inferior to Christ's Sun (Fire is not better than Water). So it is not a matter of her being required to "reflect" him. In fact, she produces the Sun, just as he sparks her. There is no question of an *imitatio* in either direction. It is rather a matter of staying with the round-dance.

In this view, the "two natures" of the "giant" are not seen as "human" (ego) and "divine" (self). Now they are sensed as mated without being assimilated (*coniunctio oppositorum*). There are many oppositions in this dance: Fire and Water, Solar and Lunar, Male and Female, *etc.*

When Christian theology with regard to the Sun and Moon is amplified in this way, the implicit psychology no longer resembles the writings of Jung in Volumes VII and IX. Rather, it is more like Jung's insights in the alchemical writings of Volumes XII, XIII, and XIV. It is akin to his insights following the dreams of 1944 and 1958 (the Yoga and UFO dreams). Jung wrote: "...it is no longer the opposites 'God' and 'man' that are reconciled, as it was before, but rather the opposites within the God-image itself."[42] The so-called "ego" is now one more piece of self, one composed of many images, each having more than one side, linked by their very opposition in a *coincidentia*, like Sun's Fire and Moon's Water, or like Moon's cool Night and Sun's hot Day. There is no "ego" in this perspective, no "I" split from a dancing-partner.

This view impinges on therapy. How often do we wish to *cure* our water-logged complexes? Or to *over-come* our dried-out lives? This would be to split off fire from water, as if their opposition were a dualism of either/or, like the divine/human split of Christian orthodoxy. But the lunar imagery of Mary, with its promiscuous pagan depth, suggests that fire and water have a more intimate and loving relationship, as if precisely in a radical psychic moisture there may be spark, and as if in the heat of soul there may be fluidity and flow.

Paracelsus said, and Jung was often to repeat, that "the Moon is the *humidum ignis*, the "fiery water."[43] The alchemical text called *Gloria mundi* puts it this way: "Sol is hidden like a fire in her water.... Seek the cold of the Moon and you will find the heat of the Sun."[44] The point seems to be not to cure or to over-come, but to enter the round-dance and to seek there the experience of opposites.

Lunar Mary's silver womb shines with the gold of the Son. As alchemist, Albertus Magnus wrote: "Gold is silver inside: silver, gold inside."[45] The Virgin is the Eros-body of Christ. Christ is the soul of Lunacy. The Fire is in the Water. The Light is in the Darkness. No Mary, no Christ! – which means: without Water, no Fire; without Darkness, no Light; without Lunacy, no embodied Soul; without Eros, no Word! No wonder the Church was reticent! It would take a sizeable faith to encompass such fundamental oppositions as constituting life's experience.

The Moonstruck Boy

Perhaps now at the end, and in the context of this amplification of the Virgin and the Moon, we may suggest a reading of the story of the Moonstruck Boy. It would begin by noting that a "sizeable" encompassing faith was just what the disciples lacked. Jesus called them *oligopistian*, "of little faith." Why?

Perhaps they thought the point was to *cure* the boy of his "lunacy," to overcome his dis-ease. This would be like trying to give him Fire, as if they possessed it, not suspecting that the Fire was already in his Water. They viewed the boy's soul-situation literally, splitting an important archetype, attempting to heal like with unlike. They could not imagine that sacred depths may already be present in everyday secular life, purity being located precisely in prodigality, male in the female, the wholeness in the disease. "The Kingdom is in your midst."[46] Their faith was not encompassing, so they did not suspect a deep incest, an erotic dance of opposition, in the lunatic nature of the boy's self. They failed by trying not to fail.

The Father gave them a clue, saying that the boy often was in the Fire and often in the Water, as if the symptom itself had purpose.[47] The disciples of Jesus likely took this literally, too, not viewing behavior also as an image of soul. "Little faith" wants it either/or. Literalism does not notice that, whether one wills or not, it is both/and.

But then how did Jesus succeed where those who followed him failed?

He spoke to the *daimon*, to the personified image of soul rather than to the boy personalistically. He addressed this autonomous power as an intimate. After all, he was a friend of things Lunar and Lunatic. The images, pious and pagan, have shown that Christ, also, was a "moon-struck" boy, his Sun hiding in Mary-Moon. He was in himself a "giant of two natures," Fire and Water, a "burning fountain."[48]

So, it was not a case of a "normal" therapist and a "crazy" patient, a Savior over against a Sinner. Rather, the situation was that of a healer who loved, not the person, but the lunacy of the "other" in himself and himself in the "other." When *he* spoke to the *daimon*, it was an inner conversation.

As Jung said: *similia similibus curantur*, "like cures like."[49]

1. Compare Psalm 121:6: "The sun shall not smite you by day, / nor the moon by night."

2. Matthew 17:14–18.

3. Compare the parallel passages in Mark 9:14ff ("he has a dumb spirit...he foams and grinds his teeth and becomes rigid") and Luke 9:38ff ("he suddenly cries out," the word for this verb being *kradzei*, cognate to our terms, "crazy," "cracked," and "crashed").
4. Deuteronomy 6:19f.
5. See: Origen, *Contra Celsum*, V. 6.
6. *Ibid.*, V. 11-12.
7. Alexander Neckam, *De naturis rerum*, I. 7.
8. Ambrose, *Exameron*, IV. 8. 32.
9. Theophilus of Antioch, *Ad Autolycum*, II. 15.
10. This phrase from ancient writers is favored by Fr. Hugo Rahner. The present essay is, in one sense, merely a report and publication of his remarkable researches which are exhaustive on the topic of the Christian *mysterium lunae*. The complete materials are found in: "Mysterium Lunae," in: *Zeitschrift für katholische Theologie*, LXIII (1939), 311-349, 428-442; LXIV (1940), 61-80, 121-131. Rahner also gave some of this in different form at the Eranos Tagung in 1944 (see: *Eranos Jahrbuch*, volume XI). One can find some of this in English in: *Greek Myths and Christian Mysteries*, trans. Battershaw (New York: Harper, 1963), Pt. I, Chap. IV (cited hereafter as "Mysteries"). Though this essay is completely in debt to Rahner for its source-work, there is an important difference of perspective. Here we are attempting to show a difference between pagan and Christian formulations which can give rise to radically distinct psychologies. This will become apparent in the penultimate section of the essay.
11. Chrysologus, Sermo, 146 (Rahner, *Mysteries*, p. 165).
12. Malachi 4:2; compare footnote #1.
13. Rahner, *Mysteries*, p. 167.
14. M. Vloberg, *La Vierge et l'enfant dans l'art français*, II (Grenoble, 1934), pp. 110f (Rahner, *Mysteries*, p. 167).
15. *Analecta hymnica*, 20 ("In rosa vernat lilium"), p. 69 (Rahner, *Mysteries*, p. 167).
16. Anastasius Sinaita, *Hexameron*, ending (Rahner, *Mysteries*, p. 175).
17. Revelation 12.1.
18. Typical are the Beatus Apocalypses and the Herrad of Landsberg paintings (Rahner, *Mysteries*, p. 164).
19. Macrobius, *Saturnalia*, VII. 16. Compare the saying of the *Zohar*, 128b: "Dew wakens the dead and is the food of the holy."
20. John Lydos, *De mensibus*, IV. 80 (Rahner, *Mysteries*, p. 160).
21. Methodius of Philippi, *The Symposium of the Ten Virgins*, VIII. 6 (Rahner, *Mysteries*, p. 162).
22. *Clavis Melitonis*, III. 6 (Rahner, *Mysteries*, p. 166).
23. This is the view of Paracelsus's *De pestilitate*, III. 95: "The moon with its light is the *humidum ignis* ['moisture of fire']." Compare the phrase, "fiery water," which Firmicus Maternus used to refer to baptismal water, in: *De errore profanarum religionum*, II (Rahner, *Mysteries*, p. 172, ftn. 4). See also footnote #43.
24. Rahner, *Mysteries*, p. 159.
25. Zeno of Verona, *Tractatus*, I. 16. 8 (Rahner, *Mysteries*, p. 174).
26. Boethius, *Consolatio philosophiae*, I. 5. 5-9 (Rahner, *Mysteries*, p. 158).
27. Firmicus Maternus, *Mathesis*, I. 4. 9 (Rahner, *Mysteries*, p. 159).

28. Plutarch, *De facie in orbe lunae*, 26-30 (Rahner, *Mysteries*, p. 159).

29. *Analecta hymnica,* 50 ("Intende qui regis Israel," strophe 5) (Rahner, *Mysteries,* p. 165).

30. Ovid, *Amores*, III. 6. 78.

31. For example: John Layard, *The Virgin Archetype* (Dallas: Spring Publications, 1972), pp. 290f; M. Esther Harding, *Woman's Mysteries: Ancient and Modern* (New York: C.G. Jung Foundation, 1971), pp. 101ff; James G. Frazer, *The Golden Bough*, Part I (New York: Doubleday, 1917), I. 36, 37.

32. I am indebted to Layard's book for this observation, though it is here used to different purpose. See: *op. cit.*, pp. 300ff.

33. Matthew 1:18b.

34. Matthew 1:22.

35. C.G. Jung, *Collected Works*, XI. 553f: "Physical is not the only criterion of truth: there are also *psychic* truths.... Religious statements are of this type....whenever we speak of religious contents we move in a world of images." Compare the statement by Joseph Campbell, "Mythology is psychology, misread as cosmology, history, and biography," in: *The Flight of the Wild Gander* (New York: Viking, 1969), p. 33.

36. Ambrose, *Exameron*, IV. 8. 32 (Rahner, *Mysteries*, p. 155).

37. Origen, *Homily on Leviticus*, V. 2.

38. See, for example, *CW*, XII: § 1-43, XIII: § 145-238. This later essay is most revealing in disclosing "a most dangerous conflict" between alchemy and the "Christian faith" (XIII: § 236).

39. Jung, *CW*, IX. 1i. 113.

40. *Ibid*.

41. See especially the essays in Volumes IX. ii and XI.

42. Jung, *Memories, Dreams, Reflections* (New York: Vintage, 1965), p. 338.

43. Compare footnote 23. This formulation was common in alchemy. The *Aurora* says: *ignis noster est aqua* ("our fire is water"). The *Gloria mundi* tells that "that which unites Sun, Moon, and Mercurius [*i.e.*, body and soul in spirit] is at once fire and water." The *Rosarium*, Philalethes, and Ripley echo this: "for in our water, fire is sought." For these and other references, see: Jung, *CW*, IX. ii. 200, 353; XI. 354; XII. 157, ftn. 31, 336, ftn. 7; XIV. 215. See also: David L. Miller, "Rhythms of Silenos in a Poetics of Christ: Images of the Great Teacher," *Eranos – 1978*, and *Christs: Meditations on Archetypal Images in Christian Theology* (New York: Seabury, 1981), pp. 143-153.

44. This is cited by Jung (*CW*, XIV. 219) who has dealt at length *psychologically* with material treated in this essay *theologically*. For example, see Jung's use of Rahner's researches in: *CW*, XIV. 28ff. In a footnote to these paragraphs Jung cites a letter which the Catholic theologian sent to him concerning Luna. Compare, in this same Volume, paragraphs 154ff.

45. Cited by Jung, *CW*, XIV. 722, ftn. 152.

46. Luke 17.21.

47. Compare the argument by Patricia Berry in: "Defense and Telos in Dreams," *Spring 1978* (Dallas), 115ff.

48. Compare the treatment of these themes in: Philip Wheelwright, *The Burning Fountain* (Bloomington: Indiana University Press, 1968).

49. Jung, *Analytical Psychology: Its Theory and Practice* (New York: Pantheon, 1968), p. 4.

The Church: Virgin and Mother

Fr. Thomas Carroll

As the title of this essay suggests, I would like to enlarge upon the image of the virgin by drawing attention to her maternal dimension. This I do for the 'community' which we are striving to image during this conference is no mere gathering of friends but a human reality imbued with a divine presence, and consequently cannot be adequately revealed by the natural image.

It is this awareness of a divine quality in the human, or the theandric nature of the Church, that renders images in their natural or simply historical significance quite inadequate as signs of the sacred. Consequently, the Christian images – and *a fortiori* the Christian sacrament–will always require a certain modification, or what might be termed more precisely a transsignification of ancient symbols. Conversely, there can be no real understanding of Christian image or indeed of Christian sacrament without a thorough appreciation of that mode of knowing which is called symbolic – that preserve of artist and poet which for so long has been shunned in our Christian West by scientist, philosopher, and theologian. By way of introduction, it is interesting to note that virginity occupied no place of importance in the religion of the Old Testament. Consequently, it comes as something of a surprise to find St. Paul advocating, as early as his first letter to the Corinthians, perhaps in the year 57 A.D., the virgin state not only as an ideal, but apparently as the norm.

But Paul must be understood against the backdrop of the fabric of faith in the early Church – namely its belief in the imminent and immediate return of Christ. Under those circumstances, one would, not surprisingly, have been occupied with the things of God more than with the things of man; and thus one can understand the rapid and indeed widespread acceptance of virginity in the early Church, long before the cult of the Virgin Mother became popular. But it was through the cult of the Virgin Mother, rather than in its widespread practice of virginity, that the Church, especially the Eastern and Western Fathers of the early centuries, came to understand the fullness of her own life and practice – not only her role as Mother but also her role as Virgin.

As early as the second century A.D., in the famous letter preserved by Eusebius, the Christians of Vienna and Lyons spoke of the Holy Church as "our Virginal Mother,"[1] a clear though implicit allusion to Mary. Similarly, an inscription in the baptistry of St. John Lateran in Rome reads that "at this spring the Church our Mother bears in her virginal womb the Sons whom she has conceived under the breath of God."[2] Patristic preaching frequently celebrated "the mysteries of the virgin Church,"[3] and St. Zeno of Verona gives the further definition that this mother who bears us without travail is still virgin after the birth of Jesus.[4] In St. Ambrose, the equation of virgin mother and Church is made quite explicit: "Like Christ's mother, the Church is wed but virgin; she conceives us virginally without travail."[5] This same theme is made with great frequency in the writings of St. Augustine, who says: "for the Church also is both mother and virgin"[6] – and he marvels at their fertile virginity and virginal fertility.

The Fathers, of course, used many other images to describe the similarities which they observed between Mary and the Church. Both are the new Eve, the tree of Paradise whose fruit is Christ, the ark of the Covenant, the gate of Heaven, the fleece of Gideon, but none of these images is our concern here. Rather, we are concerned with the image of Virgin and Mother; and it is significant that in the patristic tradition the Virgin-Mother image is never divided. Mary is never just the Virgin or just the Mother; likewise, the Church is never merely one to the exclusion of the other – for by joining them unto herself, the Church expresses the whole mystery of man's salvation. The 'word' which is in Mary is the living word of God and not the word or life of any man. It is from above and beyond, so to speak, and takes possession of the human condition for its redemption and transformation. Likewise with the Church – she is virgin, in that her gift to man is the word of God which is her very life; she is Mother, in that she bestows this divine life on her earthly children.

Such is the meaning of the Virgin-Mother image as it is applied to that divine-human community which we call the Church. As an image it reflects, on the one hand, the power of the divine over the human condition and, on the other hand, the necessity of human cooperation in the divine work of redemption or human restoration.

This point is well made by Karl Barth, the great Protestant theologian, when he writes:

> It is in Marian doctrine and the Marian cult that the heresy of the Roman Catholic Church is apparent – that heresy which enables us to understand all the rest. The Mother of God of Roman Catholic dogma is quite simply the principle, prototype and summing-up of the human creature co-operating in its own salvation by making use of prevenient grace; as such she is also the principle, prototype and summing-up of the Church. Thus that Church of man, who, by virtue of grace, co-operates with grace.[7]

Setting on one side the value judgments that go with it, I can accept the Barthian analysis because Catholic faith regarding the Virgin-Mother sums up the doctrine of human cooperation in redemption (symbolically) and thus provides the synthesis, or matrix concept, as it were, for the dogma of the Church; for as Augustine reminds us, to the degree that we understand Mary, to that degree do we understand the Church, and vice versa. Thus, just as we cannot separate the patristic image, neither can we separate Mary from the Church without destroying the biblical image.

In this context I make two observations. Firstly, I must admit that the Virgin-Mother image as depicted in patristic faith has not always been preserved in popular preaching, teaching, and piety. Under the influence of neo-Platonism, the virgin has often been presented as a sort of Platonic ideal beyond the reach of man, while the Mater Dolorosa was described in terms that completely distorted the notions of Christianity, reducing religion at times to a vulgar display of sentiment and superstition. One need only examine the prayers, the piety, and indeed the poetry of any past age –

whether it be the biblical exegesis of the twelfth and thirteenth centuries, or the love songs of the troubadors, or the preaching of the pious with the rise of the religious orders—to see that the image has been broken periodically and the balance lost; men have been divided into celestial or terrestrial figures, and precisely that truth has been lost which alone can set man free.

Nevertheless, it would be a complete distortion of history to pretend that this account tells the whole story of Mary in literature. In fact, the tendency to doctrinal aberration is much more the exception than the rule and from my survey of literature, religious and profane, I am tempted to say that the majority of writers understand the tradition perfectly well. Dante, of course, is the great example; his Mariology is sober-minded, solid, even cautious. Although he appoints Bernard, Mary's most extravagant bard, to sing her praises in Paradise, he borrows next to nothing from Bernard's writings, avoiding the great preacher's erotically rapturous tone and imagery. Instead, Dante focuses upon the orthodox theme of Mary's dignity to depict the instrument of the Incarnation which makes her man's most efficacious intercessor in heaven. Through her divine Motherhood, first of Jesus and then of the whole fellowship of the saints, Mary has won sovereignty in Paradise. In the *Purgatorio*, the princes in the flowery valley of neglectful rulers sing the antiphon, *Salve Regina*, wailing and sighing for her pity from the vale of woe. In the *Paradiso*, the gentle Piccarda Donati, driven from the cloister of her choice into an unhappy marriage, ends her tale with the *Ave Maria*, the first song Dante hears in heaven. Piccarda defined for Dante that suspension of all self that is the monastic ideal:

> E'n la sua volontade e nostra pace—
> [In his will is our peace—][8]

Her prayer to the Virgin recalls the Annunciation, when Mary also consented to the divine power and plan.

Dante thus bears witness to the growing popularity and indeed nature of the Marian liturgy of his time. But he never probes Mariological problems. He avoids what were then theological problems, preferring to work within the tradition theology had already clarified.

Secondly, we must remember that the Virgin-Mother image of the Church preached by the early Fathers depended entirely upon belief in the Virgin birth, as told in the Bible. In other words, without biblical faith (i.e., belief in the virginity and maternity of Mary, a historical woman chosen by God as a hierophany for the sanctification of man), without the explicit belief in what is called the historicity and fact of the Virgin birth, the Virgin-Mother image of the Church ceases to be an image of the new creation. In this case it becomes a 'myth' in the worst sense of the term – what Roland Barthes means when he said that "in myth, things lose the memory that they once were made."[9]

Similarly, Rene Guenon, in his rehabilitation of a symbolic understanding of religion, strays in the same direction when he concludes that Christianity is merely one manifestation of the primordial human religious tradition and consequently restricts his attention to that which Christianity shares with other religions. A Christian would argue, however, that his religion was something more than a restatement of ancient intimations of a divine presence; Christianity, he would say, is "an invasion of history by the creator of the world."[10] The cross is important in Christianity not primarily because of its symbolic qualities, but because Christ was put to death on a particular kind of wooden gibbet. The historical event came first; only later did the developing liturgy, seizing upon the approximately cruciform shape of the cross, enrich it with all the natural symbolism of the cross – its four dimensions, or cardinal points, its relation to the tree of life that gives new fruit, and so on.

On this point, I should like to refer to a recent book entitled *Alone of All Her Sex*, and subtitled "The Myth and Cult of the Virgin Mary," by Marina Warner.[11] She presents a magnificent summary of literature, sacred and profane, on Mary as Virgin, Bride, and Mother. But in her epilogue, Miss Warner compares what she calls the 'myth' of Mary in Christendom to the ancient Persian goddess Ishtar, the queen of heaven who solicits the love of the king of Uruk in the epic of Gilgamesh. The queen is rejected: her love is unacceptable because it asserts heaven's superiority and man's incapacity.[12] Miss Warner may be quite right, historically speaking, in associating the myth of Ishtar with Mary, but she makes the mistake of identifying the two; for the Virgin-Mother image of scripture and tradition asserts not only the divine love but also the human capacity, indeed the human *fiat* or response, to which Mary and the history of the Church bear witness.

At any rate, Miss Warner's book is a most exhaustive critique of Catholic Mariology which concludes with the prediction that, as an acknowledged creation of Christian mythology, the Virgin's legend will endure in its splendor and lyricism but will be emptied of moral significance and thus lose its powers to heal and to harm.

This is, I think, a legitimate conclusion for anyone to reach who has emptied the Marian cult of history and placed it firmly in the world of myth and legend; but it is not where Christian tradition places Miriam – a maid of history, chosen to be the Mother of the Savior.

You will be glad to hear, however, that in this very interesting book Miss Warner does not confine her attack to Catholic theological tradition, for she says:

> There is another sector of thought that has nothing to do with the Catholic Church, but also accepts the idea that the Virgin exists from all eternity. Under the influence of contemporary psychology – particularly Jungian – many people accept unquestioningly that the Virgin is an inevitable expression of the archetype of the Great Mother. Thus psychologists collude with and continue the Church's operations on the mind. While the Vatican proclaims that the Virgin Mother of God always existed, the Jungian determines that all men want a Virgin Mother, at least in symbolic form, and that the symbol is so powerful it has a dynamic and irrepressible life of its own.[13]

Roland Barthes pinpoints the process which Miss Warner has described when he says that "we reach here the very principle of myth: it transforms history into nature."[14]

Now I don't know whether you would share Barthes' conception of myth, but personally this view wrenches me right out of the linear Judaic-Christian understanding of time and tosses me once more into classic cyclicalism – round and round in time and ultimately going nowhere, or at very best not knowing where one is going if one is going anywhere at all.

I have no intention in this company of defending the Jungian position against Miss Warner; nor indeed, for that matter, am I qualified to criticize it. Instead I fall back upon Flannery O'Conner[15] who, in her recently published letters, makes several references to Jung. She regards him as being a greater threat to orthodox religion than Freud.[16] "Jung," she says, "has something to offer religion but is at the same time very dangerous for it, [for he] would say, for instance, that Christ did not rise from the dead literally but we must realize that we need this symbol, that the notion has significance for our lives symbolically."[17] Elsewhere in this volume she commends the German theologian Josef Goldbrunner for using Jung "in the only way he can be used, which is in helping the person face his own psychic realities," and adds that "Goldbrunner can do this because he believed in the objective reality of God." "The real religious person," she continues, "will accept the God of Abraham, Isaac and Jacob, but not one who is no more than psychic energy."[18] In her view, Jung offers the modern, sick, unbelieving world a beneficial belief in psychic realities. "This," she concludes, "is good medicine and a step in the right direction but it is not good religion."[19]

As a Catholic theologian I am particularly interested in O'Conner's comments, for there are few Catholic writers who combine a vibrant faith with a clear intellectual appreciation of this faith. "I write the way I do," she says, "because I am a Catholic";[20] and when she describes herself as "a Catholic with a modern consciousness,"[21] she means that she is "conscious in a general way of the world's present historical position,"[22] whereas for Jung, she writes, "modern consciousness" was "unhistorical, solitary and guilty."[23] Because she accepts a Catholic theology of history that acknowledges the power of Christ to direct history's very course through the Church, and in this way effect the new creation, O'Conner writes critically of Jung, who as early as 1911 said that "the Christian religion seems to have fulfilled its great biological purpose,"[24] and who later thought that "the world would save itself by outgrowing the Church."[25] For her, by contrast, "the Church is a divine institution and stands for Christ in the world" and is not to be confused with the world's "psychic energy" or "biological purpose."[26]

With this understanding of reality O'Conner transcends the religion of nature and its ritual of magic; she steps into history, into the time of the Lord, the Anno Domini, in which the face of the earth is being renewed and the signs and symbols of ancient hope, tamed and christened by the Church, are becoming new images of new things. Our Church and our Virgin-Mother image of this Church belong to this new time and to this new mode of imaging. The essence of Christianity is not to be found in any system of ethics or psychology or metaphysics or gnosis, but rather in a divine or sacred action which took place at a specific moment in time. Since the death of Socrates, men may have become better informed about the nature of reality; since the death of Christ, reality itself is wholly transformed.

Although I endorse wholeheartedly the symbolic mode of knowing and appreciate the theory of the archetype, man, however he is structured, is incapable of discovering by himself that ultimate meaning of history which I have been calling Divine Mystery, and which is brought to light in historical reality by the Spirit of God alone, and which cannot be discovered simply by the spirit of man in the realm of nature. "After all," says St. Paul, "the depths of a man can only be known by his own spirit...and in the same way the depths of God can only be known by the spirit of God. Now instead of the spirit of the world we have received the Spirit that comes from God, to teach us how to understand the gifts that He has given us. Therefore we teach not in the way in which philosophy is taught but in the way that the Spirit teaches us: we teach spiritual things spiritually" (1 Cor. 2:11-13). When this "hidden wisdom which we teach in our mysteries" (1 Cor. 2:7) is seen and believed, then the whole of Scripture, the whole of sacred history, the whole of human history become as one in the light of God's love. Conversely, confronted by the deepest experience of man's suffering and sin and by his unconquerable aspiration, we need, "not a philosophy of our age, still less of the masters of our age" (1 Cor. 2:6), but the whole of Scripture in order to discover, by the power of His Spirit, the saving Mystery of "His Hour." Without this understanding of history as "Arch-image"[27] of the divine saving Mystery, we become once more prisoners of nature's mysteries and unchristened images. We live again in a sort of twilight timelessness in which past and future are vaguely present. We see life from the other side of the tapestry, as it were, as so many unconnected, disconnected threads and it tells no story. Our Church becomes a community of men with only vague memories, our Virgin-Mother image a 'Barthesian' myth "transforming history into nature,"[28] and the gods replace our God.

1. Henri de Lubac, *The Splendour of the Church* (New York: Paulist Press, 1963), p. 7.

2. *Ibid.*, p. 202.

3. *Ibid.*
4. *Ibid.*
5. *Ibid.*
6. *Ibid.*
7. *Ibid.*
8. Dante Alighieri, *Paradiso*, 3:85.
9. Roland Barthes, *Mythologies*, trans. Annette Lavers (New York: Hill and Wang, 1972), p. 142.
10. Jean Danielou, *The Lord of History* (New York: Meridian Books, 1968), p. 125.
11. Marina Warner, *Alone of All Her Sex* (New York: Knopf, 1976).
12. *Ibid.*, pp. 333-39.
13. *Ibid.*, p. 335.
14. Barthes, p. 129.
15. Sally Fitzgerald, ed., *The Habit of Being: Letters of Flannery O'Conner* (New York: Farrar, 1979).
16. *Ibid.*, p. 491.
17. *Ibid.*, p. 362.
18. *Ibid.*, p. 382.
19. *Ibid.*
20. *Ibid.*, p. 90.
21. *Ibid.*, pp. 90, 103.
22. *Ibid.*, p. 103.
23. *Ibid.*, p. 90.
24. *Ibid.*, p. 383.
25. *Ibid.*
26. *Ibid.*, p. 394.
27. Louis Bouyer, *The Paschal Mystery* (London: Allen and Unwin, 1951), p. 38.
28. Barthes, p. 129.

Salt: A Chapter in Alchemical Psychology

James Hillman

"Some seek not gold, but there lives not a man who does not need salt" –
.Cassiodorus

I.
Towards a Substantial Psychology

Alchemical salt, like any other alchemical substance, is a metaphoric or "philosophic" salt. We are warned in various alchemical texts not to assume that this mineral is "common" salt, our table salt or sodium chloride. Yet, as we shall see, this alchemical salt is indeed common to us all – and not only as the physiological content necessary to our blood and fluids. It may well be that the epithet "common," which is curiously attached only to salt of all our everyday comestibles, reveals that salt is the substrate of what is meant by "commonly human," so that salt is the archetypal principle of both the sense of the common and common sense. Already you can see how we shall be working in this chapter: we shall be activating the image of salt as a psychological substance which appears in alchemy as the word *sal*, as an operation which yields a residue, as any of many physical substances generically called "salts," and as a property of other substances.

The word *sal* in alchemical texts, especially since Paracelsus (1493-1541),[1] often indicates the stable basis of life, its earth, ground, body. However, the term also more particularly refers to alums, alkalis, crystallizations, bases, ashes, sal ammoniac, potash, as well as to the sense qualities equivalent to these materials: bitterness, astringency, pungency, mordancy, desiccation, and crustiness, dry stings and smarts, sharpness and pointedness.

These qualities of human life belong to the very substance of personality. Indeed, the bitter and mordant qualities of personality are not only as common and basic as salt, but they are as essential to the ground and embodiment of our psychic nature as is salt itself. Our mordant, astringent, dried-out moments are not contingent and accidental; they are of our substance and essence. Although the links between salt and virginity will appear more visibly as we proceed, at least you may begin to perceive the method by means of which the links can appear at all.

This *psychological* approach to salt has two major predecessors: Ernest Jones' "The Symbolic Significance of Salt in Folklore and Superstition" (*Imago*, 1912) and C. G. Jung's richly condensed chapter in his *Mysterium Coniunctionis* (*CW 14:* §§ 234-348). The main differences between their approaches and mine lie in our different aims. Where they examine salt in a scholarly manner in order to gain an objective meaning of this alchemical substance, I am attempting to bring over to the reader its substantiality as a personally recognizable experience. Where Jung does a psychology of alchemy, I am trying to do an alchemical psychologizing. Hence, his chapter on salt, and Jones' mainly anthropological amplification, are indispensable backgrounds even though they offer less experiential closeness to the material. I intend that my speaking about salt will bear traces of salt with it.

Our model is the microcosm/macrocosm and the doctrine of correspondences between them. A man or a woman is a smaller arrangement (*kosmos*) in which all things in nature are proportionately represented. Not only is the macrocosmic world personified and alive with subjective qualities that we nowadays allow only to human beings, but the microcosm of the human being, because it is a microcosm of nature, is also a mineral, physical object, consisting of substances such as salt. The difference between this psychological substantiality and that of chemistry, which too holds that mineral and physical elements enter into the composition of a human being, is that the chemical model does not require consciousness or soul. There is a radical split between conscious subject and the physical substances. Whereas the alchemical model suggests: as within, so without. The physical world has its interiority and subjectivity because it is a larger arrangement of human nature. For alchemy, both man and world are ensouled. Sensitivity, meaning, consciousness – these are potentially present throughout.

The microcosm/macrocosm model requires a micro/macro-awareness. It asks that we feel into the world of matter with sensitivity for qualitative differences. It asks that we find in our objective experiences analogies with and metaphors of physical processes and substances.

We have lost this substantial view of personality. And because we no longer imagine ourselves substantially, we place substantiality onto the brain and bio-chemistry as basis of mind and soul. Or, we substantialize various functional and relational concepts such as instincts, drives, motives, energy, complexes, ego, repression, and the like. We cannot escape the psyche's need to imagine itself substantially, as having *physis* or being a microcosm of *physis*, even if not a gross and palpable physical stuff. And when psychology does not have an adequate language for the soul's need to substantiate, then reified substantiations spring up willy nilly.

Alchemical psychology took care of this psychic need by using a language that was both metaphorical and physical at once.[2] We know that we are not silver and sulphur and antimony – and so we can speak of ourselves as such all the while realizing that these concrete materials are also metaphorical: both gross and subtle at once. The substantialities of modern psychology – ego, drive, aggression – are conceived literally, and we forget that they are fictional constructs. So the great value of alchemical psychology is its animated language of matter, which recognizes soul in physical substance and admits the 'stuffness' of soul. It puts soul into nature and nature into soul.

Furthermore, the micro-macro model works in two directions. While endowing the world with soul, it also indicates that human nature goes through natural processes of an objectively mineral and metallic sort. Our inner life is part of the natural world order; and this perspective saves us from taking ourselves so personally and identifying what goes on in the soul with the subjective ego. Thus, salts belong to the very stuff of the psyche. *Sal* describes one of our matters, something that is 'mattering' in us and is the 'matter' with us—too much, too little salt, or salt at the wrong times and places, or combined wrongly.

Alchemical psychology describes a myriad of substances. Johnson's dictionary of 1652[3] and Ruland's of 1612[4] list hundreds of words referring to materials. These can be reduced to a system of seven basic stuffs deriving from metallic seeds of the traditional planetary Gods: all sorts of words may refer to silver, for instance, and its operations, and each of these words connote as well the planetary principle of the moon in a particular phase or guise or combination. A variety of the sevenfold system is that of three substances plus a fourth, the "tetrasoma" which itself combines four of the primary planetary metals (lead, copper, iron, and tin or antimony). The threefold system, in which salt finds a major place, derives mainly from Paracelsus,[5] the Swiss radical philosopher of nature, religious physician, and eccentric whose system of sulphur, mercury, and salt was a more subtle and chemical mode of imagining than the more gross and metallurgical model of the seven.

Because of the interrelated complexities of these substances, whatever the system, the model is polytheistic, that is, one cannot speak truly of any element alone. Whatever is said about salt is always contaminated, and must be so contaminated by the materials, vessels, and operations with which it is in interaction. Psychic materials are always in diffuse interpenetration with other materials and do not remain singly self-consistent. In fact, this very contamination is part of their definition: let us say that alchemy is soft-edged. Lines between its elements cannot be drawn hard and fast because these elements are also elementary living natures. The technique of isolation, so essential to the method of modern natural science, arbitrarily forces nature to comply with an isolating kind of consciousness and its epistemology, which cuts, separates and opposes in order to know.[6]

Alchemical salt is usually in a tandem with sulphur and what is said about salt is usually from a sulphuric standpoint. For example in Paracelsian alchemy, salt is frequently imagined as soul (sulphur as body and mercury as the spirit combining them). The illustrative image is the egg, whose yolk (sulphur) — oily, smelly, sticky and vital — is its body, whose shell (salt) — fixed, inflammable, crusty and enclosing — is its soul, and whose white (mercury) — connecting yolk and shell, mutable, slippery, volatile, changing its shape and consistency – is the egg's spirit. Or: The shell (salt) may be the body; the yolk (sulphur), the soul.

I have found that it is better to consider each component to have its own sort of body, rather than to insist that salt is always soul (or always body)[7] in a one-to-one equation. We must remember that a psychic substance does not and cannot mean one thing. So, we find that alchemists shifted 'body' to equal this or that depending on the task at hand. The same is true in our psychic work today: certain problems take on body or cry for release from body, or lose their embodiment, so that no single aspect of our psychic lives can consistently be named 'body.' As Robert Sardello has often said, body is most elusive. When body is equated with sulphur what is meant is the excitable, palpable urgency, the body of generative passions and will. When body is called salt what is meant is the fixed, consistent, stable body that encloses as an outer shell of any existent – paradoxically salt may mean its inner core: for salt was imagined by Khunrath as the center of the earth. Perhaps the best way to understand 'body' in this context is by the action of a substance: that which coagulates or brings body about therefore must itself be body. Sometimes sulphur is the coagulatory agent; sometimes coagulation is attributed to the power of salt.

The tandem of salt and sulphur continues in modern lives and modern dreams. A woman in analysis oscillates between burning enthusiasms for new people, projects, places. She is ready to catch fire at any moment, bringing a richly fat imagination and vital energy to life. She also has times of depression: drinking alone, self-enclosed, encrusted, bitter with residues of what has been, stuck for hours in a square chair at a square table, feeling low and base, sunk to the center of the earth. There is no direct connection between her sulphur and her salt. They oscillate in "mood swings." Therapeutic work, according to alchemical formula, is not to temper one with the other, but to touch both with mercury, that is, to free them from their alternating concretism by means of psychological reflection, the first step of which is to see how impersonally autonomous the swings are and how they constellate each other, as do sulphur and salt.

In another case, a young man, finding it hard to yield some of his childish innocence and the rich life in the lap of the mother and the gods, dreams first of walking with his girl through a salt desert, then of their sharing salty meat together, and then of a strange man who runs a stand on the street, handing the dreamer a salty sausage-type roll instead of what he had ordered – a roll or bun filled with yellow, sweet-cream custard. The dreamer is offended. He had wanted the savor and joy of sulphur in the sweet soft things that slip down with no effort. But the strange man-in-the-street (Mercurius himself, perhaps) hands him the bitter sting of salt that can bring tears to one's eyes. We shall now have to explore the nature of this salt.

1. Quotations from Paracelsus are from: *The Hermetic and Alchemical Writings of Paracelsus the Great*, trans. and ed. by A.E. Waite (N.Y.: University Books, 1967), 2 vols.

2. Cf. my "Therapeutic Value of Alchemical Language," *Dragonflies*, 1/1, 1978, pp. 33-42, and a sustained examination of the metaphorical, physical language of silver in my "Silver and the White Earth," *Spring 1980*, which also further differentiates the silver qualities of the moon from those in the present paper.

3. *Lexicon Chymicum* per Gulielmum Johnsonum, London, 1652.

4. Martinus Ruland, *A Lexicon of Alchemy* (Frankfurt, 1612) (London: Watkins, 1964).

5. Although a variety of salts were alchemically known in antiquity (Theophrastus, Pliny, and later Geber and Rasis), not until Paracelsus was salt elevated to one of the *tria prima*, more fundamental than the seven planets and the four elemental temperaments. Paracelsus re-founded alchemy on a tripartite scheme by introducing salt as a new third term. This 'third' position is characteristic of Paracelsus in that he held a position against both Aristotle and the Scholastics on one side and against Galen on the other. His tradition, as Walter Pagel shows ("Paracelsus: Traditionalism and Medieval Sources," in L.G. Stevenson & R.P. Multhauf, eds., *Medicine, Science and Culture* [Baltimore: Johns Hopkins, 1968], pp. 57ff.), was Platonic and Neoplatonic, especially in following the tripartite cosmo-anthropology of Marsilio Ficino – body, soul, spirit – whom Paracelsus admired. It is in his advocacy of the third principle that I see the importance of Paracelsus for Jung as a spiritual ancestor (Jung, *CW 15*, §§1-43; *Memories, Dreams, Reflections*, pp. 200, 220). Both warred against theological spiritualism on one side and empirical materialism on the other in order to hold the middle ground of soul or psychic reality. Part of the so-called 'elusiveness' of Paracelsus (O. Temkin, "The Elusiveness of Paracelsus," *Bull. Hist. Med.* 26 [1952], pp. 201-217) can be attributed to this mercurial middle ground. Although Paracelsus usually identified sulphur rather than salt with the middle integument, it was his advocacy of salt and his own saltiness (the physical, practical, common, vernacular, purgative, sharp-tongued, bitter, uncombinable nature of his personality) that shows this substance to have been as fundamental to his nature as it was to his thought. He died, by the way, in Salzburg. (On the three lines of thinking, see O. Temkin, *Galenism* [Cornell Univ. Press, 1973], esp. pp. 128-170.)

6. "Science" from *scire*, to know, is cognate with *scindere*, to cut, divide, and has the same probable root as schism, shed, and shit (as separation). Cf. Ernest Weekley, *An Etymological Dictionary of Modern English* (London: John Murray, 1921.)

7. Cf. C.G. Jung, *CW 14:* §§322-23. Salt is also the Christ, Mercurius, and thus the spirit as well as the soul, and body or earth.

II.
Salt Mines: The Mining and Making of Salt

But first – where is the salt to be found? How do we mine it, make it, prepare it. Eirenaeus Philalethes replies: "...descend into yourself, for you carry it about with you...." It is to be found in "Man's blood out of the body, or man's urine."[1] "Mark well that those bodies which flow forth from our bodies are salts and alums."[2] As there is salt in the macrocosm, so can it be mined from within microcosmic human nature. In fact, because salt is "the natural balsam of the living body" (Paracelsus: I:259) we descend into the experiential component of this body – its blood, sweat, tears, and urine – to find our salt. Jung (*CW 14:* §330) considers alchemical salt to refer to feelings and to Eros; I would specify his notion further by saying that salt is the mineral substance or objective ground of personal experience making experience possible. No salt, no experiencing – merely a running on and running through of events without psychic body. Thus salt makes events sensed and felt, giving us each a sense of the personal – my tears, my sweat and blood, my taste and value. The entire alchemical opus hangs on the ability to experience subjectively. Hence it is said in "The Golden Tract": "He who works without salt will never raise dead bodies."[3] The matters are only macrocosmic and chemical, out there, dead unless one works with salt. These intensely personal experiences which give taste and flavor to events are nonetheless common to all – both mine and yet common as blood, as urine, as salt. In other words, salt acts like the ground of subjectivity ("That which is left at the bottom of our distilling vessel is our salt – that is to say our earth."[4]). It makes possible what psychology calls felt experience. So, we must turn to this same ground to mine our salt.

"Felt experience" takes on a radically altered meaning in the light of alchemical salt. We may imagine our deep hurts not merely as wounds to be healed but as salt mines from which we gain a precious essence and without which the soul cannot live. The fact that we return to these deep hurts, in remorse and regret, in repentance and revenge, indicates a psychic need beyond a mere mechanical repetition compulsion. Instead, the soul has a drive to remember; it is like an animal that returns to its salt licks; the soul licks at its own wounds to derive sustenance therefrom. We make salt in our suffering and, by working through our sufferings, we gain salt, healing the soul of its salt-deficiency. For, as D.H. Lawrence said:

> I am not a mechanism, an assembly of various sections.
>
> And it is not because the mechanism is working wrongly, that I am ill.
>
> I am ill because of wounds to the soul, to the deep emotional self
>
> and the wounds to the soul take a long, long time, only time can help
>
> and patience, and a certain difficult repentance...[5]

The alchemical substances offer distinctions in kinds of suffering. Salt, for instance, may be distinguished from lead, in that the first is sharp, stinging, acute: it burns in on itself with wit and bite, corrosive acrimony, making sense through self-accusation and self-purification. It is purgative. Lead, however, is chronic and dense, a heavy, oppressive, gloomy suffering, without specified focus, senseless. It is constipative. Whereas the first says: "it hurts," the second says, "I can't." Where salt tastes the details of its pain by remembering precisely and with piercing agony, lead cannot see, does not know, remaining paralyzed and sunk in a general, abstract obliteration of empirical memory.

The curing of these conditions also differs: salt requires a pinch, feeling the pinch of the event that stings; lead seems to require time, that patience Lawrence speaks of, waiting it through. What results from the salt cure is a new sense of what happened, a new appreciation of its virtue for soul. The result of the lead cure is depth, weight and gravity, more fullness and the ability to 'hold it' and 'bear it.' The two contrast also in two literary genres of suffering: irony (salt) and tragedy (lead). The first tends toward common human experience while the second tends to give distance from that experience. Of course, there are "leaden salts" in alchemy, that is, conditions in which the leaden and the salty aspects of suffering are so combined that the distinctions are hard to notice: usually that which dulls and blankets the nature of salt is a result of lead. The task becomes one of separating lead from salt, black mood from recollection, poisoned spirit from subjective experience, the fateful from the personal.

Salt may also be mined from whatever is stable. As the principle of stability whose alchemical sign was a square,[6] salt can be mined from the rocks of concrete experience, those fixities which mark our lives with defined positions. These places are not merely solid facts – my degree, my property, my car accident, my war record, my divorce; these are also places where psychic body is salted away and stored. These rocks, when recognized and owned, belong to the history of my soul, where it has been salted down by the fixities of experience, giving a certain crystallization to my nature and keeping me from inflammations and volatilizations.

As salt is not flammable,[7] it seems not subject to heat: we make salt less in ardor than in recrimination, less by desire than by memory of desire. "Ash on an old man's sleeve / Is all the ash the burnt roses leave" (T.S. Eliot, "Little Gidding"). As if the ash is the memory of the fire; not a burnt-out cinder, but the fixed inflammable essence of what once flamed to heaven.

Though we do not make it by fire, we do make salt by means of dissolutions. Salt is soluble. Weeping, bleeding, sweating, urinating bring salt out of its interior underground mines. It appears in our moistures, which are the flow of salt to the surface. "During the work the salt assumes the appearance of blood" (*CW 14:* §337). Moments of dissolution are not mere collapses; they release a sense of personal human value from the encrustations of habit. "I too am a human being worth my salt" – hence my blood, sweat, and tears.

It is curious how we are fixated upon our wounds. Psychology speaks of trauma and has even invented a traumatic theory of neurosis. Why does psychology go back to the hurt child for grounding psychic development, and why does the psyche itself need to look back? It seems the soul must have its signal remembrance engraved into its psychic body so that it knows it has or is a body. Pain implicates us at once in body, and psychic pain in psychic body. We are always *subjected* to pain, so that events which hurt, like childhood traumas, force our subjectivity upon us. These events seem in memory to be more real than any others, because they carry the force of subjective reality.

Viewed from the perspective of salt, early traumas are moments of initiation into the sense of being a 'me' with a subjective personal interior. We tend to fixate on *what* was done to us and *who* did it: resentment, revenge. But what psychologically matters is *that* it was done: the blow, the blood, the betrayal. Like the ashes which are rubbed into the wounds at initiation rites to purify and scarify, the soul is marked by its trauma. Salt still is touched to the body in Christian Baptism, and eaten still at Jewish Pessach in ritual remembrance of trauma.[8] A trauma is a salt mine; it is a fixed place for reflection about the nature and value of my personal being, where memory originates and personal history begins. These traumatic events initiate in the soul a sense of its embodiment as a vulnerable experiencing subject.

The paradigmatic story of "looking back" is that of Lot's wife (Gen. 19:26). (Lot and Lot's wife were even used as alchemical terms for salt —*Johnson's Dictionary*.) Because Lot's wife could not refrain from looking back at the destruction of Sodom from which they had been saved, she was turned to a pillar of salt. Jewish commentators[9] on the tale say that her mother-love made her look behind to see whether her married daughters were following; and Christian comments on Luke 17:32 (Clement of Alexandria: *Exhort*. 94) also see the source of her move in remembrances of family and relatives, personal subjectivities of feeling. Evidently, family fixations are also salt-mines. The disappointments, worries, smarts of mother-complex love — the evening with the photograph album, the keepsakes — are ways the psyche produces salt, returning to events in order to turn them into experiences.

The danger here is always fixation, whether in recollection, childhood trauma, or in a literalized and personalized notion of experience itself: "I am what I have experienced." Paracelsus defined salt as the principle of fixation (II:366).[10] This term, like projection, condensation, sublimation, reappears centuries later in psychoanalysis where it is defined by Freud:

> Fixation can be described in this way. One instinct or instinctual component fails to accompany the rest along the anticipated normal path of development, and, in consequence...it is left behind at a more infantile stage.[11]

Here we have Genesis 19:26 recapitulated in modern psychoanalytic language. The image of Lot's family on its journey is now presented as a conceptual definition; parable becomes theory; the story salted down as science.

Among these sources of salt, urine holds a special place.[12] According to the model of the macrocosm/microcosm, urine is the human brine. It is the microscopic sea within, or the "waters below." Jewish legends[13] explain that salt is included in all sacrifices as a remembrance of the act of Creation by the separation of the waters above from those below, their having been torn asunder, and the salt remembers these lower waters and their weeping at having been cast down from nearness with God.

Urinary salts are residual traces afloat in the lower person. They are essential remembrances that betray our inner nature, its color, smell, opacity. Bladder disorders and urinary symptoms and dreams may refer to an awakening to the lower waters,[14] to the fact that there is psychic life in the lower person independent of what goes on above, and this life is an intense, burning, personal necessity which no one else can tend for you and for which time and place and privacy must be found.

Urine of the virgin boy (between 8 and 12 years) was often mentioned as a starting substance for the work. This "urine of the boy" is one of the many names for the *prima materia*. It refers to the salts in the microcosmic sea before the Fall, that is, the archetypal essence of each particular personality before it has accumulated personal residues: salt not as the result of events, but as prior to events. The virginal condition is not empty or blank, even if unsullied by experience. These salts have their own specific gravity and qualities – that is, there is an *a priori* salt in our "boy of the soul," who is defined by the fixed intensities that are the demanding urgencies of one's own particular essence. The salts in the urine of the boy are these archetypal traces of character essence, Platonic remembrances that are virginal because they are given intact with one's nature and that can only be opened by the alchemical opus.

Johnson's Dictionary states simply: "*urina puerorum est mercurius*." Of course, Mercurius' names are legion; when, however, a substance is overtly named such, there is immediate significance for soul-making. This implies that the ambitions of puer fantasy, which Freudian psychology has attributed to the urinary phase of the little boy's development, take on revelatory significance. It is not merely "urinary erotism"[15] – that I can sexually fertilize the world or extinguish its fires or start rivulets. The urinary ambition of the "boy of the soul" is also an expression of my salt, the essence of myself, my base. "Look," it says, "see my piss; this is me." There is a potent spirit to be found in the silly piss of one's little boy (even perhaps in his bed-wetting).

We can feel the primordial salt of the puer in the bitter pains of ambition that burn before any accomplishment, and also in the sense of remorse that stings before there have been external events to rue. Burning intensities can plague a childhood before worldly experience has begun, and these same salty pains reappear when the boy of the soul is constellated. In the *urina puerorum* it is a remembrance of things *a priori* that load an act in the world with more salt than puer consciousness can sometimes bear: huge guilts, high-pitched hopes, even suicide. For the puer comes not only on wings of flights and in games of love; he comes, too, smarting with a memory of beauty and what one is on earth for.

The *urina puerorum* suggests that with the right operation we can recover the salty aspect of the puer. The salt to put on the tail of puer flights is already there to begin with, if we but know the right operation for recovering it. One operation which alchemy suggests for making salt is evaporation.

The watery boy who floats in and out with the tides of emotion and follows the streams of least resistance can be fixed by the salts buried in his own tissues. These give regularities, densities, squareness, and body. When the tides of the sea are exposed to sunlight and their flow stopped, salt crystallizes; so can salt be gained by the evaporation of the microcosmic flood. For this operation, alchemists used a wide-open, flat pan; all things exposed in broad daylight and all the upward pressure allowed to escape. The steam, the smoke, and the cloudy vapors ascend and dissipate in hot air. We lose the lushness of feelings, the flush of high hopes, the dumb bogs of inertia; and, as the moistures recede, something essential crystallizes in the dry air. Here, the sealed hermetic vessel would be wrong. Evaporation means not taking events deeply and intensively but rather flattening the affects and letting a pressure steam away by itself until it comes down to itself. Evaporation to a salt: this is the common salt of the everyday table of the world which is at the same time one's own crystallized experience of it.[16]

The alchemical idea that urine contained a potent spirit, a mercurial *lumen naturalis* (light of nature) became evident in 1669 when the German, Hennig Brand – called the "last of the alchemists" – cooked urine mixed with sand and produced a soapy residue that glowed.[17] Phosphorous had been discovered. The word etymologically means "light-bringing." It is an epithet for the morning star, for Lucifer, and for Hermes. Indeed, *urina puerorum est mercurius.*

HILLMAN / SALT

1. Eirenaeus Philalethes, "The Liquor Alkahest," *Collectanea Chemica* (London: Stuart & Watkins, 1963), pp. 12-13.
2. *Museum Hermeticum* ("The Golden Tract") (London: Watkins, 1953), I:22.
3. *idem.*
4. *idem.*
5. D.H. Lawrence, "Healing," *Selected Poems*, 1916.
6. Cf. Herbert Silberer, *Problems of Mysticism and its Symbolism*, trans. S.E. Jelliffe (N.Y.: Moffat, Yard, 1917), p. 395 f. Concerning salt as square or cube, Silberer makes a nice differentiation: "Crystallization produces the regular form; fixation, the density." The scanning electron microscope shows the structure of common salt to be rather like hard-edged squares or small flat cubes.
7. On fire and salt, see Jung *CW 14:* §319. The "fire" hidden in salt is its dry power or spirit even if it remains itself inflammable. Common sodium chloride melts only at 800°C.
8. The touch of salt and bitter herbs at Jewish Passover brings back the memorial image of the Red Sea and the desert. The image must not be forgotten because it is part of what makes this day different from any other day, i.e., remembrances help differentiate and bring out significance. Salt initiates the youngest child into the bitter images of the soul. When, however, remembrance becomes more than a touch, over-salted, then "not forgetting" becomes literalized into history as facts. Then we become stuck in the past, rather than sticking to the image, and the salt is no longer an imagistic remembrance but a sign for a literalized historical experience.
9. Louis Ginzburg, *The Legends of the Jews* (Philadelphia: Jewish Publication Society, 1954), I:255; V:241-42. The same commentaries note that the destructive rain which fell on Sodom while Lot's wife was looking back on that place of lustful desire was a rain of brimstone (sulphur), i.e., salt longing for sulphur.
10. Cf. John Read, *Prelude to Chemistry* (London: Oldebourne, 1939) (1961), p. 27.
11. S. Freud, "Psycho-Analytic Notes Upon an Autobiographical Account of a Case of Paranoia," (1911) *Collected Papers* (London: Hogarth, 1946), III:453.
12. Cf. Eirenaeus Philalethes, "The Liquor Alkahest," for a short treatise on urine. For a recipe of "piss and vinegar" see *Museum Hermeticum* ("The Testament of Cremer"), II:74. The urine is to be collected from an "unpolluted [virginal] youth."
13. Ginzburg, *Legends of the Jews*, V:18.
14. Cf. Jung, "Psychological Commentary on Kundalini Yoga," *Spring 1975*, pp. 10-11.
15. H.A. Murray, "American Icarus," in *Puer Papers* (Irving, Texas: Spring Publications, 1979), pp. 91-92.
16. Since there are many salts, there are many operations to produce it, evaporation being but one. Others are calcination, putrefaction, distillation (salt as a by-product), coagulation.
17. Isaac Asimov, *The Search for the Elements* (Greenwich, Connecticut: Fawcett, 1962), pp. 35-36; cf. R.P. Multhauf, *The Origins of Chemistry* (London: Oldebourne, 1966), p. 22 f.

III.
The When and How of Salting

Physiology says that the average human body can be calculated to contain about eight ounces of table salt, and that a salt deficiency brings about convulsions, paralysis and death. As well, we need "philosophic salt."

Albertus Magnus declares: "Salt is necessary for every solution."[1] This seems a strange statement, inasmuch as we have been imagining salt as the principle of fixity, of bitter crustiness. Solutions, in contrast, seem to connote fluid, passive, receptive conditions, allowing bitterness to dissolve and crustiness to melt. The *solutio*, however, in alchemical psychology is one of the very few basic operations and because of its ubiquity throughout the entire opus, it cannot be defined in only one way. Evidently, a genuine solution must have the capacity to stabilize. It must be the embodiment of a problem and not its dissolution.

The alchemical *solutio* does not suggest simplified problem-solving. Rather, it requires salt in order to affect the matter in question in a lasting way. The salt mines of which we spoke in the last section are both deposits of salt and attempts at solution. When we sit still and sweat it out, we are stabilizing and adding salt to the solution so that it becomes a genuine one. Problems seem not to go away until they have first been thoroughly received.

The issue at stake here is the capacity to internalize, to admit and receive a problem into one's inner nature as one's inner nature. This would be to salt it. A problem reaches its solution only when it is adequately salted, for then it touches us personally, penetrating to that point where we can say: *"Fiat mihi*; all right; I admit, I give in; it's really *my* problem; it has to be." The taste of this experience is bitter, and it humiliates, and it lasts – a lasting solution.

A second use for salt is in order to "slay sulphur."[2] Remember: salt is square and blue,[3] and it coagulates. When sulphur flares up it can be slain by a pinch of salt, the pinch that kills, whether a critical eye, a sharp-tongued remark, a touch of common sense. Salt wounds and slays the impulsive reactions, because it recalls the pain incurred in similar events. Salt gives us the awareness of repetition; sulphur only the compulsion. Perhaps the exalted *sal sapientia* (salt of wisdom, wisdom of salt) is nothing more grandiose than salt's ability to inhibit sulphur.

As there are psychologies of sulphur which preach action and base themselves on desire, drive, and will, examining psychological events in terms of behavior and its reinforcement or control, so there are psychologies of salt. These tend to literalize the idea that personal suffering is necessary for every solution. They insist upon the self-improvement of interior life, upon guilt and penance and working through, upon subjective history, personal feelings, traumata. Alchemical psychology corrects this sort of literalizing by presenting the personal factor that so dominates in psychologies of salt to be impersonal and commonly general. Then, when we work at our self-correction, betterment, purification, we realize that it is not the self that is the focus of our good work; it is the salt. We are simply working on the salt. In this way the salt in alchemical psychology helps keep the work from flaming up in the inflation of personal guilt.

Salt is especially missing in young people. A young and careless man dreams of visiting C.G. Jung in his house, which turns out to be a laboratory in a huge salt-dome where a wizened Jung explains how he works on making salt. Another young man full of promise and void of accomplishment dreams of a beautiful, running deer that springs into a river, crosses, its antlers high, and then collapses on the other bank in desperate need of salt. A transition of the spirit had been made, but only through exhaustion does it come home to the dreamer how badly he needs to conserve, not only his leaping, bounding, rutting spirit, but also the experiences of his dream life where his spirit shows itself. Unless the animals of his imagination are salted they may simply vanish in spiritual heroics and aesthetic highs. Yes, we catch the bird by putting salt on its tail.

Why is young love so bitter and study for exams so bloody? Are these not rituals of the salt, ways of intensifying that thicken matters and cement them in place? Bitter love is a salt cure, curing the tender soul, with tears, recriminations, and finally, some sort of stabilized pattern. The backwards and forwards of lovers' fights between tearing passion and passionate tears enact stages of the salt/sulphur conjunction. The salt component "that just won't let go" helps preserve the relationship, when sulphur would burn it out or turn it black.

As macrocosmic salt keeps meat and fish, and pickles vegetables, so we need salt in microcosmic ecology for fixing, keeping, preserving. We can't swallow and digest all that happens in a day, or in a night – so we need long hours of pickling events in glass jars for later staring at, sharing and consuming. If we would keep something, we salt it down, salt it away. The decaying impulse of young nature – the fresher and purer the substance, the surer and sooner it rots – is held in abeyance. Salt gives us time, endurance, survival. It seasons youth by removing excess moisture, thereby preserving the soul through dryness. Dry souls are best, said Heraclitus, which Philo turned to mean: "where the earth is dry, the soul is wisest." *Sal sapientia*. Analysis shrinks.

"Salt causes matters to thicken." It acts as "knot and cement."[4] What modern psychology speaks of as "integration of personality" and "integrity of character," alchemical psychology refers to as salt, for it is this sophic substance that effects internal adhesion, knitting and knotting events into experience, shrinking generalities into specifics. Salt gives the sense of significant detail, crystallizations that pack with importance what might otherwise have been a bland evening of "waste sad time stretching before and after" (T.S. Eliot, *Burnt Norton*). We want to meet someone at the party who can put sting into a conversation. At a family affair it is usually a crusty old Aunt or Grandfather who adds the salt. The flow of unexperienced events suddenly condenses and remains fixed as we are shriveled by a penetratingly salty observation.

There is another time and place for salt: when the soul needs earthing. When dreams and events do not feel real enough, when the uses of the world taste stale, flat and unprofitable, when we feel uncomfortable in community and have lost our personal 'me-ness' – weak, alienated, drifting – then the soul needs salt. We mistake our medicine at times and reach for sulphur: action, false extraversion, trying harder. However, the move toward the world may first have to go back toward the microcosm, so that the world can be *experienced* and not merely joined with and acted upon as an abstract field. World must become earth; and this move from idea to tangible presence requires salt.

Ruland says: "Nothing can be tangible without the presence of salt." Salty language, salty wit, salty sailors, soldier's pay (salarium = salary), worth one's salt, a salted bill, a salted bitch (lustful), a dose of salts – these express the tangible values of the base, workaday, and common earth that our feet walk upon and our hands touch. This language of salt connotes each human being as "salt of the earth": only those well-born and high-placed can afford to sit "above the salt."

The mines of common experience offer this salt: the saws and skilled physical know-how of the old-timer, the age-old crystallizations of common law and common speech. Each of these is like a salt mine, and we can bring down our high-falutin' notions and half-cocked ideas by earthing them in commonality. Salt gives what one has in one's head a worth among people: tangible value on earth. Commonality needs to be distinguished, however, from being practical and finding application. To earth an image is not to sell an invention. Rather, to salt or earth one's winged speculations is to express them with a common touch; tangibility of style.

Earth is also a local sense. There is salt in local speech: accent, patois, the idiotic or idiomatic. Whether one-liners that are grainy epitomes or drawn-out tales that meander across the land, local speech makes words tangible. The difference between dialect and dialectics, between patois and jargon, between earthy humor and dirty joke, between local idiomatic and national idiotic (televisionese) is all a matter of salt.

"Salt is not added in equal portions to every kind of food; and this circumstance should be diligently considered by the physician" (Paracelsus, I:264). Now, we are talking about dosage. Salt requires particularizing; it forces one to take note of the specific taste of each event. Tangibility means recognition and discrimination of specific natures. This sheds a new light upon the idea of the common: it is evidently not merely collective and general; what is common, however, is a sense for the particular – the water in this village is softer and sweeter than the water on the other side of the valley; these game birds need to hang another day; you can't use that kind of nail in this kind of wood; when the fever turns into sweating, you have to give even more liquids. Paracelsian medicine turned to the patient and tried to make acute differential perceptions; yet it also tried to be a medicine of and for the common people in earthy dialect. We have perverted the meaning of "common" to denote *all*, or *usual*, or *equal*; whereas "common salt," alchemically speaking, refers to the sharp perception of inherent natures which brings out their individual properties so that we can understand the right dosage.

As we become salty, the caution of salting tends to reverse. Where once it was necessary to catch the bird and conserve experiences, we begin to find ourselves slowly pickling in brine. Events don't let us go: they return to our heart's blood, leap with tears to the eye, bring us to break out in cold sweat over a past deed, burn in the bladder. (Paracelsus speaks of the "evil there is in salt" [I:259].) No longer the conscious application of salt, salting now becomes autonomously psychic. The soul forces its tangibility upon us and brings home our common and base susceptibility to human pain. Perhaps this is the eros of salt Jung writes about, or the wisdom of it, or the black earth and shadow associated at times with salt in alchemy; or perhaps it is the ashes and dry earth to which we are returning, the soul's essence becoming fixed, intimations of immortality that first feel like personal pain.

Paracelsus writes (I:43): "Salt corrects and fixes leprous Luna, cleansing it from its blackness." So, salt is also a "corrective" – and particularly a corrective of lunatic nigredo conditions by fixing them. A bitter despair, a drawn-out moody meanness, a corrosive worry, a stubborn self-ignorance are leprous. These conditions eat into their own skin, and one picks at oneself. These conditions make the reflective power, which belongs with Luna, splotchy, coming out only in spots, here and there, tatters of whiteness that leprously perpetuate the condition rather than clearing it. Although "leprous" in alchemy generally meant "impure," Paracelsus seems to be speaking of a sickness of reflection itself, when the powers of the moon become sicklied over, Hamlet-style. Rather than having the body of a clear insight, such reflections attack one's own embodiment – my actions, my nature, my self.

Salt corrects this illness of reflection by means of fixing precisely what it is that is wrong. The blackness refers to the generalized stain obscuring reflection, those introspective attempts to see into the dark that only further darken the mind. The acute attack of salt particularizes the mental state by means of a precision of feeling. Exactly what, when, where, and how must be felt, so that the "general mess of imprecision of feeling" (T.S. Eliot, *East Coker*) can be spotted, and each spot cleared one by one. The larger disaster is corrected by the smaller sense of it. Accuracy means acuteness, and it brings pain the correction of salt. The running-on of reflection in its wasting-away spottiness and self-eating leprosy can be purged by salt.

A woman dreams of a small, bottomless lake of salt and there are warnings to stay out of the water. She falls in and the water is so thick that it doesn't feel liquid. A long piece of salt catches her right arm and begins to pull her under. With effort she disengages from it and manages to climb out by getting toe-holds in crevices of solidified salt along the bank.

Public, collective opinion warns against what it sees as a bottomless salt pit of depression. But she falls in, despite her opinion and intention. And when she is in this lake, it is so dense and thick that the water no longer flows on. Stuck. (Salt causes matter to thicken, says one of our texts.) Here this thickening is like the process of identification: she has become immersed in the thickness of her suffering – which at the same time is the place of her becoming more dense, stable, and solid. One piece of this generalized lake of salt, one crystallized moment of it – a remembrance, a guilt, a bitter point of pain – catches her arm of action and pulls her further inward and downward. Disengagement happens by effort, particularly by finding toe-holds in already memorial, crystallized experience, from which the moisture has dried out. She can actually make her way out by standing upon what she has already been through. She is afforded a way out of the bottomless lake by standing on a solid 'bank,' by 'banking' on something solid that is there whenever the bottomless lake is there. Like cures like: the disengagement from identification with salt takes place *not* through the efforts which only drag her further under (not of the right arm), but through small basic understandings that can be found in the little depressions and faults (crevices) of her solidified subjective experience.

1. Albertus Magnus, *Libellus de Alchimia*, trans. by Sister Virginia Heines (Berkeley: University of California Press, 1958), p. 61.
2. *Museum Hermeticum*, "The New Chemical Light" (Michael Sendivogius), I:154–55.
3. Allen G. Debus, *The English Paracelsians* (London: Oldebourne, 1965), p. 163: "Salts are proper to blew colours." (Reference to Edward Jorden's *Discourse of Naturall Bathes, & Mineral Waters* [London, 1631]). Jorden also wrote probably the first treatise in English on hysteria.
4. D.R. Oldroyd, "Some Neo-Platonic and Stoic Influences on Mineralogy in the XVI and XVII Centuries," *Ambix*, 21 (1974), p. 148. (Reference to Nicolas Le Fevre – 1615-1669).

IV.
The Fervor of Salt

Our account has attempted to bring home the experience of salt in alchemical psychology. We have come to see that as the ground of subjectivity, its nature is to fixate, correct, crystallize and purify, all of which it can do to subjectivity itself. This purification of subjectivity shall more particularly occupy us in this final section where the connection more clearly emerges between salt and virginity.

We have already met its hard and square, densive-protective nature. For example: the egg analogy of Paracelsus, where salt was the shell; and in the writings of Joseph Duchesne (Quercetanus, late sixteenth century) where salt appears in the hard matter of things, their roots, bark and bones, those parts that are clotted, cemented, coagulated, or congealed.[1]

We may go so far as attributing to this substance that tendency in writings about salt to conclude with a clotted thought, a reduction to a basic idea. The multiple nature of salts, their multiple origins and effects, that the term refers to so many different qualities of experience and chemical materials (alums, alkalis, ashes, etc.)[2] — all tend to congeal into a single basic principle. For Jones this idea was "semen"; for Jung, it was "Eros." The stuff of which we write becomes the stuff with which we write and we are affected by the material we work with. As we would take in the reader, captivating and convincing, so does the material, because it too is ensouled, capture our imagination: we lose mercurial volatility and sulphuric richness and become reduced ourselves to repetitions, moral constraints and fixities of expression as we attempt to go ever inward toward the pure roots and bones, the crystallization of that experience called *"sal."* The importance of salt as value (expressed above in terms of soldier's pay) instead becomes an overvaluation of either the place of this substance within the alchemical opus or of one's interpretation: an overvalued idea due to an overdose of salt.

This effect of salt proceeds from its own fervor, a fervor of fixity which can be distinguished from the fervor of sulphuric enthusiasm and its manic boil of action, as well as from the fervor of mercury and its effervescent volatilism. Salt's fervor is rather holy, cleansing, and bitter; immovably fixed; fanatic.

You will recall that Paracelsus (I:258) held that we eat salt to cherish our nature of salt and that we desire salt for its own sake.

Salt desires itself. Its appetite works in us and through us for itself. It is fixed upon itself. Where sulphur and mercury are found in and by means of other events, salt is the experience of feeding on experience. By closing out the other principles it can intensify its own interiority. A salt mine right there in whatever we call 'mine.' Thus, *in extremis*, salt eats into its own nature, corrosive as lye in its own self-reflective purifications: recriminations, repentance, ashes, lustrations toward an ever-purer essence. Its suffering is self-caused. This is the salt that turns all reds to blue—blue in the senses of cold, puritan, celestial, exclusive, loyal, doleful, deadly (cyanide, prussic).[3]

Here we may review those images of pure salt that we have already seen: of the virgin boy's urine, white crystal, final ash. Here, too, belong the images of the salt desert as if it were heaven: the Elysian fields, a Dead Sea, celestial, immaculate, and barren, a crystalline ground of self-laceration, that sense of being grounded in long-suffering nobility, which negates even the *fiat mihi*. For nothing comes from the Great Salt Lake when one has oneself become purely salt, like Lot's wife. As salt fixates and purifies itself, suffering becomes fanaticism.

The intensity of this fanaticism appears in alchemical language both as ammonia, caustic soda, alkali, white lime, and as natron, the white salt of niter which is a destructive, explosive powder. (Even table salt is a delicate crystallization of a lethal gas—chlorine—and a highly flammable, unstable metal—sodium.)

Some alchemists recognized as salts whatever appeared in crystalline form. May we imagine that a salt crystallizes to bind its inherent fervor? These fanatical salts manifest themselves more in political and doctrinal affairs, although similar attitudes appear as well in the concretistic *askesis* of paranoid schizophrenia. The very virtue of salt—its down-to-earth, concrete commonality—seems only a virtue in combination with other elements. Alone, salt fixates on itself, attempting to become the pure elixir which alchemy insists is always the result of many combinations.

The inherent capability of salt to crystallize its own lethal volatile essence is what I would call the inherent virginity of salt. By virginity here I mean the self-same, self-enclosed devotion to purity. I believe it is this aspect of salt that is alchemically associated with the cold, hard aspect of Luna, the woman as "bitch."[4] The Luna-sal connection is discussed at length by Jung, who considers salt another term for the moon, another manifestation of the more general principle of "the feminine."[5]

In Rome, salt was indeed the province of the virginal feminine, the Vestals.[6] They prepared the sacrificial animals and sprinkled each with salt to make it holy. The Vestal (i.e., an initiated and ritualized) Virgin was the mistress of the salt; she understood how to handle it. Here is the virgin, not in the fervor of fanaticism, but the virgin as mediatrix; she knows the right dosage, a pinch, a touch, a grain, not a state. Jung quotes Picinellus: "Let the word be sprinkled with salt, not deluged with it."[7] The dosage of salt is an art: it must be taken *cum grano salis*, not corrosive, bitter irony and biting sarcasm or fixed immortal dogma, but the deft touch which brings out the flavor. Even the salt of wisdom (*sal sapientia*) and the salt of common sense become crystallized and destructive when taken alone, squarely, or imagined straight, for it is in the very nature of salt to literalize itself and conserve itself into a crystal body. Any insight or experience preserved as truth or faith becomes virginal: it closes into itself, becomes defensive. Too much salt. We are each virginal when we are preserved from experience by preserved experience.

Hence the importance of the Vestal Virgins. Like cures like. Their conscious virginity enabled them to handle the purifying power of the salt. As initiates in the cult of salt, they must have understood the dangers of its "corruptive ferment."[8] Society is always in danger of the fervor of salt – puritanism, fanaticism, terrorism – and the preservation of Roman culture depended upon the Vestal Virgins.[9] This suggests that a psychological understanding of the power of salt and its dosage is necessary for the human body, the soul's body, and the body politic. Too little and principles go by the board; too much and a Reign of Terror ensues.

We can recognize when the principle of fixation has become a fixation of principle. Then salt is unable to be combusted and released by sulphur or is unable to be touched or stained by mercury: neither life nor insight possible, only dedication, barren and pure. Alchemical psychology protects itself from salt by its composite thinking, mixtures, a bit of this and a bit of that, where its salt is always yielding its body to sulphur and mercury, to the love for it of spirit and soul, *fiat mihi*, let it be done to me, receptive to other powers, touching them and in touch with what it is not, the alien and unredeemed. For the function of salt is not its own conservation, but the preservation of whatever it touches. Images of the Virgin Mary, welcoming the alien, letting all things come to her and affording protection by giving her body to whatever their condition, by giving that touch which brings out their flavor and blesses their earth – this presents the soluble salt, Stella Maris. For as Arnold of Villanova said, "The salt that can be melted" is the desirable salt.[10] "Prepare this salt till it is rendered sweet."[11]

As a final example of the fervor of salt, or what the alchemist Khunrath[12] imagines as a hell fire in the midst of salt, perhaps a too-bright light in which purity burns with a consuming passion, let me close with an 'alchemical text' by D.H. Lawrence from his novel *The Rainbow*,[13] the chapter called "First Love."

The scene is set among haystacks under the moon, at a wedding feast. Images of fire and darkness pervade, and those familiar alchemical opposites appear when "red fire glinted on a white or silken skirt."

The principal figure, Ursula, "wanted to let go."

> She wanted to reach and be amongst the flashing stars, she wanted to race with her feet and be beyond the confines of this earth. She was mad to be gone. It was as if a hound were straining on the leash, ready to hurl itself after a nameless quarry into the dark.

She invites Skrebensky to dance. "It was his will and her will ...locked in one motion, yet never fusing, never yielding one to the other."

> As the dance surged heavily on, Ursula was aware of some influence looking in upon her.... Some powerful, glowing sight was looking right into her.... She turned, and saw a great white moon.... And her breast opened to it.... She stood filled with the full moon, offering herself.... She wanted the moon to fill in to her, she wanted more, more communion with the moon, consummation.

Skrebensky takes her hand and wraps a big dark cloak around her, and they sit. She desires desperately to fling off her clothing and flee away to the moon, "the clean free moonlight." Skrebensky, too, takes on a metallic quality, "a dark, impure magnetism. He was the dross, people were the dross."

> Skrebensky, like a load-stone weighed on her.... He was inert, and he weighed on her.... Oh, for the coolness and entire liberty and brightness of the moon. Oh, for the cold liberty to be herself.... She felt like bright metal....

And her hands clench "in the dewy brilliance of the moon, as if she were mad." Then a strange rage fills her and her hands feel like metal blades of destruction. "Let me alone," she said. She throws off his dark cloak and walks towards the moon "silver-white herself."

They begin again to dance and a struggle starts between them. She feels "a fierce, white, cold passion in her heart." And though he presses his body on her, as if to make her feel inert along with him, there remains in her body a "cold, indomitable passion." "She was cold and unmoved as a pillar of salt."

To him she feels "cold and hard and compact of brilliance as the moon itself," and he wishes to set a bond around her and compel her to his will.

> They went towards...the great new stacks of corn...silver and present under the night-blue sky...the silvery-bluish air. All was intangible, a burning of cold, glimmering, whitish-steely fires. He was afraid of the great moon-conflagration of the corn-stacks.... He knew he would die.

Ursula becomes aware of the power she holds: "a sudden lust seized her, to lay hold of him and tear him and make him into nothing." Her hands feel hard and strong as blades and her face gleams "bright and inspired."

Skrebensky again draws her close to him:

> And timorously, his hands went over her, over the salt compact brilliance of her body.... If he could but net her brilliant, cold, salt-burning body in the soft iron of his own hands.... He strove...with all his energy to enclose her, to have her. And always she was burning and brilliant and hard as salt, and deadly.

He puts his mouth to her mouth, "though it was like putting his face into some awful death," and her kiss was "hard and fierce and burning corrosive as the moonlight...."

> cold as the moon and burning as a fierce salt. Till gradually his soft iron yielded, yielded, and she was there fierce, corrosive, seething with his destruction, seething like some cruel, corrosive

> salt around the last substance of his being, destroying him, destroying him in the kiss. And her soul crystallized with triumph, and his soul was dissolved with agony and annihilation.

I have let D.H. Lawrence present the figures and scene of my conclusion for several reasons. First: to exhibit again the connection between psychology and literature and to suggest, even, their interchangeability. Second, to bring witness to the ever-presence of alchemical imagination – in this case the conjunction imagery of *sal et luna* as sulphuric iron and salt. (I do not believe we can reduce these images and this rhetoric to the influence upon Lawrence of his father, a miner, or of the mining milieu of his native place.) Third, to show personalities as composed of and carried by imaginal substances – metallic seeds, chemicals, impersonal minerals, the hard and enduring natures of the Gods working through our wills. And, fourth, to raise a veil and sound a warning concerning so-called lunar consciousness.

We have been moving into a new moon-worshipping time: right-sided brains and left-handed cults; moon magic; intuition, occultism, astrology, herbals, and witches; nudity and the untrammelled body; pop-visions of Our Lady; Artemis freedoms, Diana power, Lesbian politics. A new lunacy as sanity. "The Feminine" as a fervor of salt.

Too close to the moon can be madness. "Love burns in changes of the moon." Says Robert Duncan, "She comes so near to earth / And makes men mad. / O misery!"[14] We watch this moon too close to earth in Ursula, whose lunacy is a death-dealing fanaticism, bitter, assertive, caustic, sterile, corrosive, salt. We witness Ursula's body turning to salt as she becomes infused with her subjectivity. Like Lot's wife, she is self-occupied. Because salt is the soul of the body, it can reach us through body-subjectivity. We become pure body-experience, and transmute the event of the other into only an instrument of the experience. Thus the body turns to salt; it remains untouched even while it is being embraced, because no event is happening, only the intense experience of subjectivity.

There is a confusion here between the urge for purity and the desire for liberty. The Vestal Virgin submitted utterly; there was no possibility of imagining liberty together with purity. The result of this confusion is a fervid and lonely purism, a vestigial virgin without her ritual and isolated from her cult, burning with divine eros, yet seeking the white light for herself, her devotion to the moon poisoned by the salt of subjectivity. "People were the dross." Purism is the salt in the soul that allows no recovery: "Carthage shall not rise again." Virginity as utter destruction.

Each planet, each worship, each archetypal perspective has its kind of terror. So there is a terror in the moon, in the purity of a single-minded devotion which its salt can claim. The terror arises not just from its so-called dark side, from Lamia, and Hecate's bitch, or Lilith, but from the moon's sway over the salt in the seas and our microcosmic flood. From the analysis in this chapter we may understand purism as the fixation of salt by itself into a literalization of the preservative principle. Owing to the special relation between Luna and Sal, purism is the main danger in our contemporary devotions to the moon. To invoke the moon is to invite the salt[15] – and unless we are trained in the nature and power of salt, as were the alchemists, we may become unwitting terrorists of the night, bending iron through fanatical devotion to singleness, free of the other, against the core-existence of the other, alone. Ursula has not been trained in alchemical psychology where one learns that the moon is not a stopping place. The alchemical model considers it a way-station to the other planets as the microcosmic moon, the psyche, implicates various gods.[16] The moon implies the others, so that in an alchemical psychology devotion to them can never become usurped by the salt it activates: it can never be virginally singleminded, because the devotion necessarily extends to what the moon reflects.

The first symptom of fanaticism is purism or virginalism which we have come to understand indicates a hyperactivation of the salt and a loss of the mediating principle of dosage. We each need a Vestal Virgin to guide our hand in apportioning our fervid dedication and the grains of inherent bitterness which accompany dedication and give it its zest. The very same salt that is wisdom, truth, common sense, wit, and subjective feeling is also salt the destroyer. Dosage[17] is the art of the salt; a touch of the virgin, not too much. And this dosage only our individual taste and common sense can prescribe. Only our salt can taste its own requirements.

1. Debus, *The English Paracelsians*, p. 94, quoting Joseph Duchesne, *Le Grand Miroir du Monde*, Paris, 1595.
2. For a treatise showing many salts and the different operation for each, see R.R. Steele, "Practical Chemistry in the Twelfth Century: Rasis de aluminibus et salibus," *Isis* 12, (1929), pp. 10-21. (Rasis' practices are reported by Bonus of Ferrara, *The New Pearl of Great Price* [London: Stuart & Watkins, 1963], pp. 366-371.)
3. For a rich phenomenology of blueness, see William Gass, *On Being Blue* (Boston: Godine, 1976), and my piece on "Alchemical Blue" in *Sulfur,* I/1, ed. Clayton Eshleman, Pasadena, 1981.
4. C.G. Jung, *CW 14:* §§ 174 ff.
5. *Ibid.*, §§ 234, 240, 320-355.
6. Stephanie Demetrakopoulos, "Hestia, Goddess of the Hearth," *Spring 1979*, pp. 65-68, with notes. Cf. for details of the preparation of the *mola*, Georges Dumezil, *Archaic Roman Religion*, trans. Ph. Krapp (Chicago: University of Chicago Press, 1966), p. 318.
7. Jung, *CW 14:* § 326.
8. Eirenaeus Philalethes, "The Liquor Alkahest," p. 22.
9. Cf. Demetrakopoulos, "Hestia," p. 68.
10. Jung, *CW 14:* § 240.
11. *Museum Hermeticum* ("The Glory of the World"), I:177.
12. Cf. Jung, *CW 14:* § 337; *Museum Hermeticum*, I:176-177.
13. D.H. Lawrence, *The Rainbow* (1915) (New York: Penguin Books), excerpted from Chapter XI; other passages exhibiting saline, lunar, metallic metaphors, and even a chemical view of personality, in the relationship of Ursula and Skrebensky, appear in Chapter XV, "The Bitterness of Ecstasy."
14. Robert Duncan, "A Description of Venice," from *Poems 1948-49*, Berkeley Miscellany Editions (Glen Gardiner, N.J.: Libertarian Press, n.d., courtesy of the Author).
15. One name for salt was the "common moon" (*Museum Hermeticum*, I:177). The affinity of *sal* and *luna* was metallurgically experienced in the process of gold-making: when salt is added to a gold/silver alloy and exposed to red-hot heat for a period, the salt and silver conjoin to form silver chloride which is absorbed by the walls of the crucible, letting the gold run free. The gold is then washed with hot brine which absorbs the silver chloride, purifying the gold. R.J. Forbes, *Metallurgy in Antiquity*, 2nd ed. (Leiden: Brill, 1971), p. 180.
16. Jung, *CW 14:* §§ 217-18.
17. It was Paracelsus and his school (A.G. Debus, *The English Paracelsians* [London: Oldebourne, 1965], pp. 32-35) that "went to great pains to determine the correct dosage with their medicines." The concern with dosage derived most probably from the iatrochemistry of mineral and metallic salts as specific medicines. If the Paracelsians taught the art of dosing salts, salt was the principle that taught the Paracelsians (see note 5, Part I above).

Afterword

Gail Thomas

All this, and the virgin evades us still. Why is this image so elusive? Just at the moment when we seem to catch her she is gone again. Just when understanding seems clear—the "a-ha!" moment—it becomes suddenly unclear. Now we have it, now we don't. Like Actaeon, who meets his death when he gazes at the forbidden form of Artemis, the light goes out for us just when we seem to have the virgin image clearly in focus. The notion of virginity remains oblique and ambiguous.

Strange that this puzzlement should remain, especially after working closely with the images of virginity in literature, art, myth, psychology, and theology as they have been presented by the writers of essays in this volume. After such a wealth of material, one would expect to have the notion clearly in command.

The difficulty seems to lie in the nature of the image itself. The image is contradictory: 'whole within itself'; it speaks of fecundity and new possibility and at the same time implies impregnability, sterility, existence in solitude and isolation. Such a contradiction makes it hard to hold on to the notion of virginity; it is rather like those contradictory three-dimensional drawings that jump from one perspective to another, even as we gaze at them.

One argument would proffer that to be virginal is to be 'untouched' by experience. This understanding sheds light on the phenomenon of being unable to stay with—spend time with—the virginal image. Tom Moore provides an important dimension to the figure of virginity in his description of the tapestries at Cluny in France. These extraordinary works of art reveal how the virgin seduces the unicorn (which, as Dr. Moore suggests, images spirit in action). The virgin sits isolated within an enclosed garden – a protected space – and that quiet repose lures the unicorn. When the unicorn rests contentedly at the bosom of the virgin in this place of solitude, death makes its appearance. The hunters lie in wait for this moment and take advantage of their helpless prey.

Seen from the perspective of the virginal as untouched by experience, virginal isolation lures the spirit, nursing it at its breast. But at that moment, death comes to the spirit. High-horned impulses and drives become static within a protected and isolated place. At the very moment when highly-charged ideas meet pure and unviolated nature, there is death to the spirit. Spirit wants to move, to mediate between spheres. Seen as isolation, the virginal remains intact, uncontaminated. This condition Patricia Berry calls "resisting the image." To resist the image is to be virginal in psyche, and to be a psychic virgin is to be closed to the image. The virginal, she suggests, is a fantastic, personal, and simplistic quality of mind: fantastic, when much seems to happen yet little actually occurs; personal, when perception works only on itself; simplistic, when a psychological state lacks complexity.

In this view, the place of the virginal is isolated; it is frighteningly lonely, cut off from the rich encumbrances of the world. It is like the image of Endymion, as described by Rafael Lopez-Pedraza, lying sleepless in a sleep-like state, eyes open, undreaming, waiting for visitation from the moon-goddess Selene. Sequestered in this sterile state, the virginal psyche waits. This extreme virginal place creates a void, a vacancy far removed from the fecund, regenerative forces of life. Lacking imagination, enduring without hope, imprisoned within a fixity, the virginal psyche waits. It waits without hope, like the image of the virgin sitting in the garden *before* the unicorn comes to her. Little wonder that as Moore says, "there is something deadly devious in the virgin's lure." The virgin carries within her an inherent danger – the deadly void, vacuous isolation, insular privation.

Psychologically, this experience of penetrating the virginal realm may be felt in the fear of breaking a silence, speaking the first word, or in the fear of new ideas. The fear of committing ideas to paper, or in uttering them publicly, and the fear of making choices which define and delimit our existence may reflect the trepidation with which the spirit approaches the virgin. The virgin lures the spirit. The lure calls to our attention how we long to speak, to write, to take a stand, but also how much we fear the isolation or loneliness involved in making our position known. The virgin's lure becomes destructive when the notion of being 'whole within oneself' is taken literally so that the word spoken, the word written, or the stand taken isolates and makes one's position impenetrable.

What, however, is spirit seeking when it nurses at the virgin's breast? Moore says: "The virginal nourishes the spirit, while the spirit makes the virginal psyche pregnant."

Certainly, there is more to virginity than a deadly lure. The image does, after all, encompass the entire divine order of the feminine, from Artemis and Athena to Aphrodite and Hera, all acclaimed with the epithet 'Parthenos' – reason enough for our confusion!

While concentrating on the fantastic, personal, and simplistic qualities of the virginal, Berry nonetheless offers a way of working with (or re-working) the virginal image. She suggests that the virginal can serve to recover the nature of a thing itself. How would this be possible?

What is called for is a radical view of the virgin, that is, a return to the root metaphor of the virgin as 'whole within itself.' The virgin as 'Parthenos,' child of the unmarried mother and therefore unfathered, suggests an undeniable inner authority, an integrity, a being complete within oneself. No search here for paternity; the virgin as 'Parthenos' stands intact with spirit self-contained. Any patriarchal claim would come as an invasion, as if by a foreign power. The virginal realm seen as 'Parthenos' and manifested by the great matriarchal images of western culture, maintains its own integrity. It becomes the numinous, housing the sacred, nourishing the spirit. It is, as Robert Sardello suggests, like a sanctuary, an inner room of the temple where a transformation brings instinct into union with soul.

David Miller suggests that salvation is from the virgin. The Virgin as Moon reflects the divine light of Christ as Sun. Dr. Miller's claim that "it is in this way we can have divine light in our world" because "we would not be able to take it in direct doses," also helps to clarify the attraction of the virgin's lure. The virginal as mediator of the divine light does not diminish the integrity of that sphere; rather, it enhances it. It is the divine light that entices spirit. And it is the virginal which heals, nourishes, and replenishes the spirit. As Fr. Thomas Carroll reminds us, the Virgin Mary forms a major part of the Patristic tradition in the Christian Church. Mary offers "the Word of God," Logos, the Divine Light, "which is her very life." She carries the Divine mystery within her being. Mary is the image of virginity undivided. She contains, heals, nurtures, and forgives without loss of integrity or particularity.

It is towards this realm that Louise Cowan guides us through Faulkner's imagination towards "the completion of himself for which man yearns" but for which there can be no satisfaction. The virginal realm – as imaged by the inviolable woods, by the anchorite teacher, and by Venus, Kore, and the prostitute – is described through the theme of desire and abnegation, illuminating the powerful transformation which re-works instinct (in Layard's sense) to become what we might come to call culture. We are led to see that it is homage to some sacred mystery that lures the spirit to the virgin. And the virginal invariably induces a suffering which precipitates a new order. Faulkner's fictional world allows us to see the virginal (ironically, through a complexity of images) in its own particularity. By concentrating on the theme of "non-consummation," Dr. Cowan illumines an essential aspect of the virgin's ambiguity. Through the characters of Isaac McCaslin, Eula Varner, the young Artemis figure Pat Robyn, the fecund Lena Grove, and the prostitute Everbe Corinthia, we become aware simultaneously of the massiveness of the symbol and of the particularity which the virgin nature reveals.

Images in dream, art, architecture, and literature are important to this volume of essays. The images give it body. The unicorn nursing at the virgin's breast, the lady dancing in front of the bulldozer, Endymion lying in a waking sleep, Isaac McCaslin witnessing the manifestation of the ancient bear, the rites of passage in the Eleusinian Mysteries, all bring forth recollection, identification, subjective experience and a sense of the personal. James Hillman would call these the "salt" of this volume. The salt is the essence of one's self, the way one identifies one's special character. The virgin 'salts' experience, like psychic trauma or bodily hurt. "Trauma is a salt mine," says Hillman. "It is a fixed place for reflection about the nature and value of my personal being, where memory originates and personal history begins." The danger in virginity is fixation, being rendered immovable in a rigid or sterile condition.

We may entertain one more image of the search for the virgin. The musical *Hair,* which exploded into American life in the 1960s, called attention to the cultural shift toward greater embodiment but also suggested the need for a simultaneous move toward an inner domain. In the haunting words of the song "Donna," we learn of a "once upon a time" time, a "looking for Donna" time. Donna was a sixteen-year-old virgin.

> Oh Donna, Oh Donna, Donna
> Looking for My Donna.

Sung repeatedly throughout the song, this refrain becomes "Looking for MaDonna."

The musical would have us believe that the image of the madonna, or of the sixteen-year-old virgin, is an image for which we yearn even in the midst of the most carnal or fragmentary experience. We experience the virgin, not only when we are isolated in nature, but also when we forgetfully live our busy everyday lives. It is as if the virgin calls us *to* ourselves, to be true to something within ourselves which cannot be shared with others. The musical speaks with cultural reflection about a theme easily recognized as universal and archetypal—the need for integrity, for particularity. Culturally, it can be experienced in what Sardello calls "an initiation more deeply into the body, a bringing together of Demeter's earth body with Persephone's psychic body."

The images and characters in these writings reveal something primordially essential about human nature. That which we call 'the feminine' serves as container for the mysteries of life. Embodied imaginally in the virgin, these mysteries remain unpossessed, unmarried, and unfathered. The images of virginity bring to us a sense of integrity in the midst of a technological world. At a time when the feminine is subdued by masculine dominance, a recovery is required: 'modes of being' whether the Amazon, the Mother, or what Nor Hall calls the 'medial woman' which regain for us the prefigurings of a feminine order. To be virginal within these modes of being is to remain purely within them, to give oneself over totally to them, to be encased by them, *imaginally*, so that there can be a recovery of one's own integrity, one's own unique particularity. This seems to me to be the virgin's milk.

The Incest Taboo and the Virgin Archetype

John Layard

1.
Introduction

Two-fold purpose of the taboo

As a tribute to Professor Jung's life-long work on the *anima* and on the archetypes associated with it, I propose in this essay to put forward certain conclusions that can, I think, legitimately be drawn regarding the origin and two-fold purpose of the Incest Taboo, and on the problem of Virginity to which it gives rise. While agreeing with Freud in rejecting the popular notion that the incest taboo had any hygienic motive such as the prevention of in-breeding on biological grounds, or indeed any theory that would presuppose a definitely conscious purpose, I shall nevertheless part company with him in his interpretation of the anthropological data; and shall suggest that, far from being due to an Oedipus Complex which arose at a comparatively late stage in the growth of civilisation, the taboo owes its origin to the sacrificial principle which aims, so far as human affairs are concerned, at the ultimate transformation of instinct into spirit. This is itself, however, but a second stage following on the preceding and complementary opposite creation by the spirit, represented by the Word, of instinct called in biblical language the Flesh.

For an account of the first stage we have to rely mainly on Scripture and primitive mythology and on our own ability to interpret them. For the second, however, we have sure anthropological evidence, and it is to this that I propose to devote the major part of this paper, showing how the incest taboo has both a manifest and a latent purpose, both of which (as in dreams) are unknown to the conscious minds of those who put the taboo into practice, and particularly to the majority of ordinary folk for whom the word "taboo" and its world-wide equivalents appear often to have a purely negative meaning. For, like most laws whether written or not, the taboo says only what you may *not* do, and as such has simply to be obeyed, whereas it is the task of those seeking to probe into the inner meaning of things to try to find out what is the positive purpose behind it.

What I therefore propose to do is to examine first, very briefly and with biblical assistance, the hypothetical condition before the taboo came into existence, and then to follow the course of its two divergent and complementary opposite results, which are:

a) the manifest result in terms of primitive social organisation, with special reference to the very early so-called "class" or "sectional" systems of kinship; this is the problem of the "*anima* without", that is to say the *anima* externalised in the form of a wife; and

b) the latent and ultimate result in terms of the psychological or spiritual effect which kinship organisation produces in the psyche of individual men, in other words the realisation of the "*anima* within".

This contrast I propose here to illustrate by means of biblical analogy in terms, on the one hand, of the physically pregnant Eve representing the externalised *anima* in the form of the actual wife together with the projections made by the man upon her, and, on the other hand, of the spiritually pregnant Mary, the Virgin, called by the Church the Second Eve, who represents the internalised *anima* or positive mother-image within the psyche.

And as it is the development of this latter which I believe to be the real aim of the whole process initiated by the taboo, this will inevitably in turn lead on to a discussion of the inner meaning of "virginity", which in its spiritual sense is the ultimate goal towards which the incest taboo leads, demanding as it does the highest possible development of the transformed sexual instinct in terms of the union of the soul (considered always and in both sexes as being female) with God. This inner meaning of virginity I shall then illustrate by means of dreams dreamt by members of both sexes showing how "virginity" on the psychological or spiritual level is quite independent of the presence or absence of virginity in the flesh, and may on the one hand result in the complete inner unity or spiritual pregnancy of the priestly celibate or on the other hand in physical pregnancy in cases in which this has not previously been achieved.

Eve the negative anima projection, called the "diseased will"

If spiritual virginity thus leads to successful pregnancy, it is clear that the whole subject of the incest taboo is highly paradoxical. Thus, it is worthwhile noting that both Old and New Testaments begin by a complete reversal of the order of nature, though in opposite directions. Thus, in the Old Testament, when God made Eve out of Adam's rib, woman was born from man instead of man from woman. The motif is repeated in Jeremiah, 30, 6, when the Lord says: "Ask ye now, and see whether a man doth travail with child?" The question was in each case: What sort of woman did he bring forth? Was it a positive *anima*-image or a negative one? Jeremiah is foreshadowing the positive one. In Adam's case, however, that which he brought forth became the temptress, for the first thing she did was to deceive him by rebelling against God and dragging him with her out of paradise. Then Eve bore fruit, and the daughters of Eve increased, till one of them, Mary, reversed the course of nature again by conceiving without a man; and whereas Eve became the mother of men, Mary the Virgin became the mother of God.

Who then, psychologically speaking, was Eve the tempted and the temptress, and who was Mary the untemptable? Eve the proud who brought disaster on mankind, and Mary the humble who brought salvation?

I cannot, I think, do better than begin by quoting on this subject from the remarkable sermon of St. Bernard called *De Conversione*[1], in which he describes the negative *anima* or what he calls the diseased "will" in terms of an internalised Eve, referring to her as "that lady" who "lies at home paralysed and grievously tormented" (p. 14) and who, when commanded by the reason to amend her ways, "leaps forth in her fury, forgetful of all her weakness. With dishevelled locks, and with torn garments, with naked breast, scrabbling at her ulcers, gnashing the teeth in her parched mouth, infecting the very air with her poisonous breath, she exclaims: Why is not the reason ashamed of such an attack, such an onslaught upon the wretched will? Is this, says she, all your conjugal fidelity? Is this the way you feel for me when I suffer so much?" (p. 15). And, having enumerated all her faults, he goes on, "For it is thus with the soul; as there is the memory which is befouled, so there is the will which befouls" (p. 17), and ends up "Reduce to meekness the wild motions of the will, and make it thy care to tame the cruel beast. Thou art bound to the will; strive to relax the bond which thou canst not break. The will is thy Eve..." (p. 19).

What then is the proud Eve, thus produced out of Adam's body, but the projection of the *anima*, bringing with it indeed children peopling the earth, for unregenerate nature cares not for the soul, but bringing at the same time all the ills that are described by the holy Father in this Rabelaisian manner which is so refreshingly different from the polite milk-and-water Christianity of modern times? On the contrary, the humble Mary brings forth no merely human children, but shows forth the Second Adam reborn phoenix-like out of the ashes of the First. Psychologically speaking, just as Eve is the *anima,* both in the flesh and as a negative projection in the personal unconscious, so Mary represents the wholly inwardised positive *anima* or mother-image in the impersonal unconscious.

For this, Mary pays the price according to Catholic doctrine of having no ordinary human children[2], nor even a human mate (for Catholic theology has it that Joseph also remained a virgin, whence his position of patron of celibate orders), while Eve, for her human mother-hood, pays the terrible price that both Genesis and St. Bernard describe.

Divine incestuous union before the Fall

But the earth has to be peopled, or there would be no people to save, so Eve as well as Mary has her positive function. What their respective functions are in the psychology of man I now hope to show in anthropological terms through a study of the problem of

Incest Taboo, which will be found to be very different indeed from that put forward by Freud and based on more exact anthropological data. For, in the Garden of Eden, Adam was as yet within the womb in blissful union with his mother and in the innocence which was also the ignorance resulting from lack of any contact with what is called the "world"; he was given up to an uninterrupted contemplation of all the mysteries of creation, being himself the material embodiment of it and of its inner processes; a creature without pride not yet launched out into that ocean of affairs in which man must himself become biologically a creator and so suffer the temptation (which was Eve's, directly handed to her by the serpent) of thinking himself "like God", in other words of acquiring the imperious will which was Eve's and so landing himself in the condition of inflation which leads to outer darkness.

This state of one-ness with the mother while yet within her womb, typified by Adam and Eve in Eden, is the epitome of incestuous union with which all life begins, and also to which it must return, though on another plane. But between this alpha and omega, this beginning and this end, this First Paradise of Eden within the maternal womb and the Second Paradise of New Jerusalem within the womb of God, there lies a wilderness in which complete separation must be made from the first as *sine qua non* of entry into the second. And this wilderness is life, conscious and active life overhung by the shadow of death; in which the loneliness of the path of personal individuation is either shirked because the spiritual umbilical cord keeping a man tied to his earthly mother is never wholly cut, resulting in every kind of negative projection, or else this task is accepted to the best of a man's ability, whereby the union with the internal *anima* or positive mother-image is gradually formed, leading in turn to the soul's brideship with God to whom the *anima* herself acts as a bridge, thus leaving the individual free to conduct life without negative projections due to undue and unrealistic dependence on human love.

Basic nature of incest desire. Taboo not instituted on biological grounds, but is a sacrificial system with both manifest and latent content.

This inner conflict, common to all men, is reflected in the organisation of human society by the tremendous taboo placed on incest by primitive peoples – I say tremendous because it is, with them, a matter of life and death. All society is based on it, and without it no society would exist. Nevertheless the misconceptions in the modern mind about the real meaning of incest are so great that we are ourselves in danger of carrying on incestuous unions in the form of negative *participations mystiques* without knowing it; and, indeed, much neurosis is itself the result of such psychologically though not necessarily physically incestuous unions.

Freud says (it may be taken that this is the corner-stone of his teaching, and it is one which no serious psychotherapist would dispute) that the incest desire is fundamental in man. Thus he says, "Psychoanalysis has taught us that the first object selection of the boy is of an incestuous nature and that it is directed to the forbidden objects, the mother and the sister" (*Totem and Taboo*[3], p. 28). Further, "The basis of taboo is a forbidden action for which there exists a strong inclination in the unconscious" (*ibid* p. 54). He also says, "The law only forbids men to do what their instincts incline them to do.... Instead of assuming therefore, from the legal prohibition of the incest, that there is a natural aversion to incest we ought rather to assume that there is a natural instinct in favour of it" (*ibid* p. 205).

These statements, bold in their day, are now commonplaces of all psychological analysis. It is our task to ask ourselves why, if this desire is so imperious, such a taboo should ever have grown up.

The usual explanation, so usual that it is implicit in the thinking of almost every modern person and particularly of those calling themselves "scientific", is that it is due to the biologically harmful effects of in-breeding. This view, however, does not tally with the facts. Freud himself, referring to both men and animals, says that "the harmful consequences of in-breeding are not established beyond all doubt even today and in man they can be shown only with difficulty" (*ibid* p. 206); and also, "it must be pointed out that a prohibition against in-breeding as an element weakening to the race, which is imposed from practical hygienic motives, seems quite inadequate to explain the deep abhorrence which our society feels against incest" (*ibid* p. 207). This is so true – although apparently unknown to Freud – that one of the outstanding anthropological facts, as I shall shortly show, is that the incest taboo as practised among most really primitive people is *not only designed to prevent in-breeding, but in many cases carries with it obligations that actually promote it*.

The first thing to be quite clear about is, therefore, that contrary to all modern habits of thought and popular belief, in-breeding is not biologically harmful. If such a belief were true, it would be true also of animals, which it manifestly is not since all specialized and so-called "pure" breeds are based on it. There are indeed cases, such as small isolated communities, in which Europeans are said to have become degenerate through in-breeding, but these are not proved and many other factors enter in, such as extreme poverty, which are very frequently ignored. There is, on the other hand, the positive evidence to the contrary of the innumerable isolated or semi-isolated communities in which in-breeding is not only practised but has continued to be practised for countless generations all over the world, not only today but also in the past, with no such negative results. Those tribes which have practised it have been so strong as to have borne the whole brunt of primitive man's struggle to lay the foundations of civilisation, and to maintain these against all the disintegrating forces of nature.

If biological reasons were not the prime causes of the taboo, what was? Freud's hypothesis, as advanced in *Totem and Taboo*, is that of the primitive horde led by an aged patriarch who possessed all the women and whose sons finally rebelled, killed him, and married his wives, thus giving rise to the so-called Oedipus Complex. This has done more to discredit Freud among anthropologists than any of his works, since there is no evidence whatever that such a condition ever existed, and the misinterpretation of anthropological data on which it is based is well known. Incidentally, this purely subjective myth is a fascinating one when regarded as a reflexion of Freud's own psychology, and, taken symbolically, represents an unconscious rebellion against his own patriarchal and over-intellectualised attitude as represented by the father.

This is not to say that the Oedipus Complex does not exist, or that it does not hold a prominent place in the personal unconscious of modern man. But it is not found to anything like the same extent among the very primitive. Its formulation as a basic dogma of psychoanalysis appears to me to result from the view expressed in another of Freud's statements, "Taboo is a very primitive prohibition imposed from without (by an authority) and directed against the strongest desires of man" (*ibid* p. 59). That it is indeed directed against man's strongest desires is not in dispute, but that it is imposed ultimately from without I should dispute strongly, since analytical psychology can demonstrate from dream material that the ultimate source of the taboo lies within and is a dictate not of the personal unconscious but of the deeper levels of the collective unconscious, and only has to be enforced from without (*i.e.* by the collective conscious) when the deep inner sacrificial truths mentioned below are lost sight of.

I have risked tiring the reader by quoting these well-known passages in order to show just how far we can go with Freud, and where we part from him. For, to him, the ultimate authority appears to be external, whereas for us it is internal. We know that the ambivalence found in the psyche may not be solely due to external causes nor be essentially negative at all, but is to be found deep down in the very nature of life and as the very mainspring of our being, becoming negative only if thwarted by us, but being in the nature of illumination if it is not. For the maxim that nothing exists outwardly that did not previously exist internally is fundamental to Jung's teaching.

If, then, the authority imposing the taboo is internal: What is it, and Why is it? The answer requires a teleological understanding, not an aetiological one. Aetiologically every kind of reason could be adduced, as every neurotic adduces aetiological rationalisations for all the ills that have befallen him, but the wise analyst seeks the reason not in the past but in the purpose, assuming that every ill is due to a misunderstanding of that purpose.

For the ultimate purpose of everything in life is always sacrifice, which means transformation, the transformation of something "natural" into that which is "supernatural", that is to say not less but still more natural than biological nature because on a "higher", or as we should say "deeper", level. For there is nothing in nature that is not there in order to be transformed, and it is a universal phenomenon that the "natural", which always starts off by being "good", inevitably becomes regarded as "bad" if or when it does not submit to transformation. That is why the Latin word *sacer*, from which our "sacrifice" is derived, like its Polynesian equivalent "taboo" carries with it the double connotation of "unclean" and "holy", indicating the "uncleanliness" of that which resists transformation and the "holiness" of that which is transformed. Freud recognises the ambivalence of the concept (queer only to the modern mind but fundamental to the primitive), but curiously enough misses its import. For the fundamental meaning both of *sacer* and of "taboo" is "set apart", and what is set apart is regarded as "unclean" only by those who do not understand the meaning of transformation, but is recognised as being "holy" by those who do. For every instinct has to be satisfied, but there are two spheres, that of the flesh and that of the spirit, which are complementary opposites in the sense that what is forbidden and indeed may be deadly in the flesh can and must be satisfied in the spirit, so that, in the words of the gospel, "all things may be fulfilled".

Jung treats the question with regard to the incest wish not, as Freud does, by saying that the desire for the mother on the part of the adult is a negative thing that has to be avoided, but that on the contrary it is a positive thing that has to be followed up at all costs until its meaning becomes clear and it can therefore be re-integrated as a positive spiritual factor into conscious life.

We are now in a position to turn to primitive man, and to ask ourselves the following questions:

1. If incest is not biologically harmful, in what way is it so harmful that primitive man regards it as a cardinal sin?
2. This being the case, why, after forbidding marriage between a man and his mother, sister or daughter, do the prohibitions against lesser degrees of incest vary so greatly from place to place, and why should many primitive peoples not only permit but actually insist (as I shall show) on marriage between first cousins?
3. Why, after all this apparent care against in-breeding, should there be special religious occasions set apart in which, as sometimes happens, all these regulations are suspended and complete license allowed?
4. Why, when ordinary men and women live normally under this strict and mortal taboo, should the gods they worship and the culture-heroes they admire and hold up as patterns of life, so very frequently (and especially where the taboo is strongest) be believed to have married their mothers, sisters or daughters?

The answer is, in the first place, that the taboo is not directed against in-breeding, but arises from reasons of quite a different kind, which will be seen to explain all these apparent anomalies and show that they are not only not anomalies but follow logically from what its purpose is.

2.
Manifest Purpose of the Taboo: The "*Anima* Without", Leading to The Expansion of Society

The purpose of the incest taboo has, as I have already mentioned, a manifest aspect and a latent one.

To take the former first, its manifest purpose is "civilisation" in its most literal sense, that is to say, the enabling of men to live together in amity and in a condition of mutual co-operation.

Systematised in-breeding among Australian tribes. "Cellular" or "closed" kinship systems.

To illustrate this, I propose briefly to examine the known and carefully tabulated facts concerning some of the tribes on the Australian continent. These tribes, or hordes as they are called, for they are mostly food-gatherers often restricted to fewer than 200 members, have a social organisation of great apparent complexity, rigorously enforced through the action of age-long public opinion, the expression and conservation of which rests with the older members of the tribe. This unofficial and unformulated governmental power of the older men is of greater importance than is usually understood. For we are ourselves so used to quick changes in the social system brought about partly by the huge size and manifold interests of modern communities, changes often imposed from above or through the action of outstanding personalities, that we find it difficult to conceive of their absence. In primitive communities all these factors are absent. The social horizon is restricted to a few hundreds of people and has been so for countless centuries. There are no chiefs to wield arbitrary authority, nor do the extremely limited possibilities allow of the emergence of anything in the nature of what we now call "reformers". Indeed, as I have emphasised in another work[4], a really primitive community resembles an individual person in the sense that its members are all one. They are in the first place all closely related to one another, so that the action of one has immediate repercussions on all the others. In the second place the solidarity of these tiny groups in the face of natural forces as well as enemy tribes is of such over-riding importance that any major departure from the accepted order is highly dangerous to the delicate balance on which the whole tiny structure depends, and is therefore punishable by death. This balance may be compared not only to the external balance of the human frame but to its internal balance also, the balance of glandular secretions or the structure of cells. Indeed, the "cellular" analogy is such a close one that, as will shortly be shown, the social organisation of Australian tribes is, like that in many parts of the world, based on a primary division into two moieties which split first into four, then into eight sections (and elsewhere into six or twelve) in a manner closely similar on the one hand to that of primitive biological organisms, and on the other hand to the sub-divisions of the individual psyche[5], and the smooth interaction of all these interlocking parts is essential to the survival of the tribe.

I therefore propose first to examine the origin of the cellular organisation itself, in order then to demonstrate the gradual emergence of the social (that is to say the manifest) organism out of the biological, and then how in its turn the social aspect inevitably gives rise to the latent spiritual or psychological aspect.

But before proceeding with this I must once more make it quite plain that, with regard to the incest taboo, in all probability neither the ultimate social aspect nor yet (and this is quite certain) the ultimate psychological aspect is present in the minds of the natives, or at least to the rank and file. The typical misconception that man rules his own destiny (in the vulgar sense of knowing with any kind of exactness what he is doing) is to be seen in the opening pages of Freud's study where, discussing the apparently complicated regulations associated with the taboo, he says that they "seem to spring from legislation with a definite aim in view"[6]. In the first place such a concept as legislation, which is the result of definite planning, is utterly foreign to the primitive mind. And in the second, following from it, it cannot be emphasised too strongly that the forces which rule men's lives are not conscious in this kind of way, that man is not "captain of his fate", but that he is, on the contrary, part of a scheme of growth and development of which, since he is part of it, he cannot know the end, and which of its own power forces him to find out by a ceaseless process of trial and error what is the path that he is meant to tread. Further, this path is never revealed to him in direct terms, but always under the appearance of material fact concealing a spiritual purpose behind the prompting on the material plane.

To take the former or material plane first, envisage man the animal or, more important still, woman the animal, guarding her brood against all comers, jealous and murderous against any who should approach them, her mate providing the food and aiding in the defence. No social life could come of that. The brood grows up. Either the boys, after the "gang" stage, return and mate with her or with their sisters, or else they start other families with strange females who will be equally hostile in defence of theirs.

No human beings are known to live like this, for no human beings live without some kind of social life, and for social life two things are necessary.

It is not enough to rear children and defend them until they are old enough to defend themselves. There must be co-operation as well as defence. The easiest form of co-operation would clearly be within the family unit itself, through in-breeding which is not biologically unsound. But in-breeding has one effect, often thought to be biological but really cultural, namely that not only does no new blood enter the family, but also no new thoughts. Methods of food-gathering will be stereotyped, as also will methods, if any there be at this stage, of providing the shelter so necessary for any cultural advance. Culture-contact is essential to progress. But so also is a measure of peace. Therefore "new blood" must be brought in, not for the sake of the physical "blood", but for the pooling of new experience based on a common need. But it must be "new blood" which is not hostile. And as all primitive life is based on kinship the new mate must be: (a) unrelated for the sake of the pooled experience, and yet (b) related for the sake of peace.

Marriage with the mother's brother's daughter.

How can such a paradoxical demand be fulfilled? To the primitive mind there is no paradox, for every man has two parents, but under the very primitive conditions in which knowledge of physiological paternity may be entirely lacking there is only one obvious parent demonstrable by means of the senses, and that is the mother from whom the child was born. Therefore, when seeking for a mate, a man does not take any woman from any unrelated group (such a practice is almost unknown), but, on the contrary, he goes (or did in early days almost all over the world) to his natural protector, that is to say not to his father who in matrilineal communities is often only a visitor, but to his mother's brother, and says, "Uncle, will you give me a wife?" And Uncle says, "Why, yes, you can have my daughter", whereupon he marries his *mother's brother's daughter*, who is his first cousin on his mother's side[7].

This arrangement fulfills both conditions. For the wife, who brings in the new blood, is in terms of kinship, both *related* to him on his mother's side, which means peace and family solidarity, and at the same time is *not immediately related* to him on his father's side and thus brings to his family unit the new trains of thought and experience which she has derived from hers.

It thus becomes not only *permissible* but, as the resulting social organisations become stabilised, also *obligatory* over a large part of the world's surface, for a man to marry his mother's brother's daughter or first cousin on his mother's side; and this is today, and has been for countless centuries, the prescribed marriage in most parts of Australia and in innumerable other parts of the world. In biblical times it was the marriage which Isaac (Gen. 28, 2) commanded Jacob to make with the daughters of Laban, his mother's brother, of whom Rachel the younger was his beloved and gave birth to Joseph. As though to emphasise the divinely incestuous nature of this union, on Laban's meeting with Jacob the latter is expressly referred to as his sister's son, and Laban exclaims, "Surely thou art my bone and my flesh" (Gen. 29. 13, 14). But at the same time the second condition of acquiring new experience was also fulfilled, since Laban "lived in a far country", whither Jacob had to go and work for Rachel for fourteen years before Laban consented to their union. For real incest is of the mind, not of the body, and the purpose of the incest taboo is to prevent a negative *participation mystique*, which is not of the blood but of the spirit. Every man nowadays who has, as we figuratively put it, "married his mother" has contracted an incestuous union though there may be no blood relationship between him and his wife. In spite of this we pride ourselves that we are not incestuous because we don't marry our sisters nor yet, with rare exceptions, our cousins; though here it must be added that this latter reference is to town-dwellers only, since healthy country stock in small village communities everywhere were, until the advent of strangers due to improved communications, to a very large extent in-bred.

However this may be with regard to Europe, it is the case that marriage with the mother's brother's daughter, that is to say with the first cousin on the mother's side, is and has been the basic form of marriage for countless centuries for at least a third of the world's population.

Dual Organisation and the 4-section kinship-system

But this is not all. For, among many people, the degree of consanguinity prescribed between married people has been still greater in some once wide-spread cases, in a manner which I will now describe. For, while among certain peoples this system based on each man marrying his first cousin on the mother's side has not been what is called a "closed" or circumscribed one, that is to say that it spread outwards, in the sense that the wife's brother, while himself also marrying his mother's brother's daughter, found her in another group, in other cases this form of marriage was combined with what is called the *Dual Organisation* of Society into two exogamous *matrilineal moieties*, to one of which every member of the tribe belongs and from the other of which he must take his wife. These moieties are themselves highly symbolical of the fundamental dichotomy both of external nature and of internal psychological structure as mirrored in the social organisation of the tribe, as may be seen from the names by which they are known. Hocart[8] thus lists the pairs of moieties in such widely-separated areas as Australia, Melanesia, South India, North and Central America, Siberia and Ancient India (and many other areas might have been cited), in all of which almost exactly contrasting names for the two moieties are used, such as: Light and Dark, Sky and Earth, Day and Night, Seaward and Landward, Noble and Lower, Big and Little, Right and Left, Gentle and Rough, and Male and Female (despite the fact that each moiety is made up of both sexes), and in which, though the prescribed inter-marriages preclude the possibility of special characteristics inherited through the blood, nevertheless the members of the two moieties are held to be recognisable respectively by the contrasting character-traits symbolised by their complementary-opposite names. Now, all native transactions, whether of barter or in the presentation of foods, goods or ritual courtesies or any other things, are characterised by the equality of exchange, and the more primitive the community the more exact the correspondence in kind. This also applies to marriage, giving rise to what is called *sister-exchange marriage* whereby when a man marries a wife he gives in exchange his own sister to be married to this wife's brother.

Now, in a kinship system based on the Dual Organisation in which each man marries his mother's brother's daughter and also gives his sister to be married to his wife's brother, and where this double transaction is repeated from generation to generation, the very important result automatically occurs that the wife, who is on the one hand the *mother's brother's daughter*, is on the other hand *also* the *father's sister's daughter*, thus:

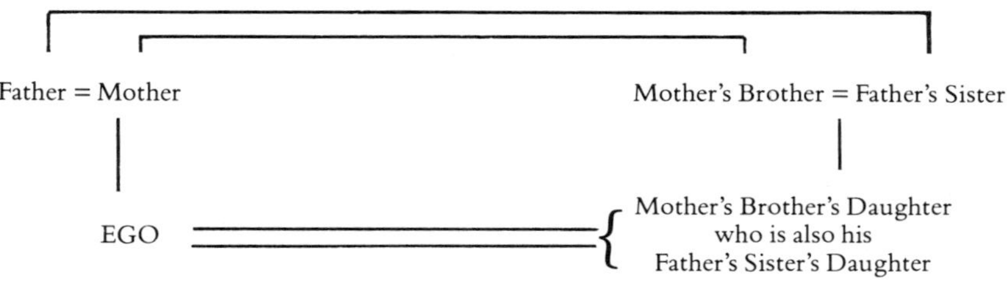

Fig. 1.
To illustrate "cross-cousin" marriage

In other words, in such a system, each man marries his first cousin not only on his mother's side but also on his father's, so that the incest-at-one-remove is doubled.

There is no space here to elaborate on all the implications of such a system, and I can only refer the reader to my book *Stone Men of Malekula* (chapter V), in which it is shown that in Australia, despite the overt patrilineal organisation of individual hordes and the great distances and innumerable linguistic barriers that divide them, the matrilineal moieties in fact cover the whole continent and form the fundamental bond underlying the whole kinship structure. The effect of this customary form of marriage repeated over countless generations is, in each horde that practices it, the *automatic* formation of two *patrilineal moieties* also. And these patrilineal moieties cross with the matrilineal moieties in such a way as to create locally (as for instance among the Kariera in West Australia) what is called

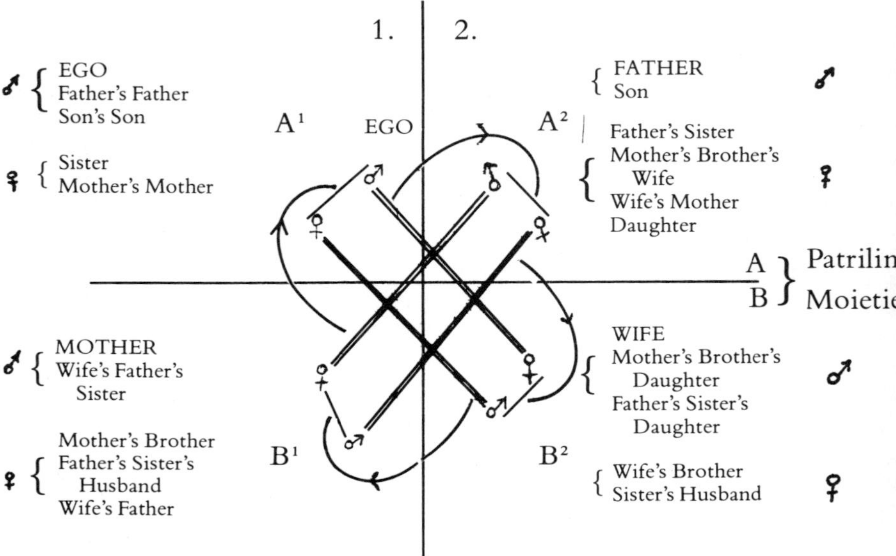

Fig. 2.
4-Section Kinship System.

Matrilineal moieties in vertical columns 1 and 2. Patrilineal moieties in horizontal columns A and B. Each of the four quarters so formed represents a marriage section. Male and female signs ♂ and ♀ represent *all* men and women in a given section, in which each man marries his MBD who belongs to the opposite matrilineal moiety *and* to the opposite patrilineal moiety from himself. Curved descent lines lead from each marriage to the children of that marriage, who belong to the matrilineal moiety of the mother and to the patrilineal moiety of the father. Thus a man of A^1 marries a woman of B^2 and their children are A^2, but his sister's children are B^1.

(From *Stone Men of Malekula,* Fig. 20, with kind permission of Messrs. Chatto and Windus.)

a *4-section kinship system*, a kind of primitive "cellular" organism which is at one and the same time *endogamous* in that it is completely self-contained, and also *exogamous* in that no man ever marries a woman who belongs *either* to his own continent-wide matrilineal moiety *or* to his own local patrilineal moiety.

This is the simplest of so-called "closed" kinship systems, of which the preceding diagram is a schematic representation.

Although it may seem complicated to us, it is very simple to the native, and while for an adequate explanation of it I must refer the reader to the above-mentioned work, it will be seen that the diagram does in fact include all possible relationships and, which is vital from the native point of view, shows how the entire population of the horde (which it must be remembered may not number more than 200 members) falls into four groups or sections, from only one of which (that containing his mother's brother's children) a man is allowed to select his bride.

To those of us who think in terms of internal psychic attitudes corresponding to external relationships, the implications of this "cellular" social organism interpreted in terms of the psychological structure of each individual composing it will be seen to be very great. To take one instance only, I may point out in passing how the four chief figures in the psychological drama of life, namely Ego, his Mother, his Father and his Wife, all fall into different sections, and that a preliminary discussion of these in terms of the four psychological functions will be found in an article entitled "Primitive Kinship as mirrored in the Psychological structure of Modern Man" (*British Journal of Medical Psychology*, Vol. XX, Part 2, 1944, pp. 118-134).

Expansion beyond the limits of the 4-section system.

If the above brief account has any lesson to teach, it will be that the prevention of biological in-breeding as such is very definitely *not* the reason for the incest taboo, but that, on the contrary, its object is the expansion not of biological but of social contacts. That is to say that, by forcing a man to marry outside the immediate circle of his own biological family unit, he is thereby brought into contact with a wider group of related persons all having mutual obligations towards one another and therefore pooling their diverse experiences and discoveries, as well as building up a primitive social unit for purposes of mutual protection and the solidarity of the group.

So far, however, the group thus achieved is a very small one. For what countless ages it remained on this secure but limited basis we do not know. The next phase, so far as Australia was concerned, consisted in doubling its size. But it must not be supposed that any primitive community did this "on purpose". Till man can find some way of discovering what nature intends him to do and of doing it in a straightforward way, the means by which advances are made will continue to be by way of quarrels about what seem essentials but are in fact only means to an end. The best explanation so far put forward as to the social mechanism by which this new advance was made is that suggested by Professor Radcliffe-Brown who puts it down to the age-long problem of the mother-in-law, taking in this case the form of the extreme awkwardness, which the 4-section system entails, of a man's wife's mother being at the same time his father's sister. Now, among the rules of avoidance that accompany the incest taboo is that which prohibits a man from speaking to, or having any direct communication with, his *wife's mother*, since she belongs to one of those categories of women with whom there is a temptation to mate, but with whom at no cost must this be allowed to happen. But if the wife's mother is at the same time the *father's sister*, in a patrilineal community such as the Australian horde, she is, until marriage, a member of Ego's own camp, and even after her marriage is a frequent visitor to it. The problem then becomes how to find a wife who can still be reckoned as a kind of "mother's brother's daughter" but does not bring with her this very awkward problem.

The solution[9] actually found is that a man, instead of marrying his first cousin on his mother's side, marries his second cousin on that side instead; in other words, instead of marrying his mother's brother's daughter, he marries his *mother's mother's brother's daughter's daughter*. This effectively removes the embarrassing situation I have mentioned, since this relative's mother is no longer necessarily also the father's sister. This is the *manifest* reason for the alteration in custom. But the *latent* reason (and therefore the ultimate cause) is that it brings about an enlargement of the whole social system, and actually (as described on page 116 of my above-mentioned book) causes each of the patrilineal moieties to split, thus giving rise to *four patrilineal descent groups* instead of two, which, combining with the two matrilineal moieties which remain constant, lead to the expansion of the former 4-section system into an *8-section* one. This is the system which has been most thoroughly investigated among the Aranda of Central Australia. In this expanded system the incest barrier is also extended, and marriage with the mother's brother's daughter which in a 4-section system was not only allowed but prescribed, now becomes looked on as being as incestuous as having intercourse with the mother or sister, and not only marriage but any kind of relationship with her is punishable by death.

Elsewhere, as in parts of Melanesia, it is the *mother's brother's daughter's daughter* who becomes the prescribed bride producing a *6-section system*, and there is evidence that in the Chou period in China the system had expanded into a *12-section* one[10].

It is, incidentally, of interest to note that every "closed" system of this kind is a repetitive one. Thus, in a 4-section system such as has been depicted in Fig. 2, while a man's children must inevitably belong to a different section from his own, his sons' sons return to his own section every two generations. This rotation of what are called "sociological equivalences" varies, however, with the characteristics of particular systems. For example, in a 6-section system formed of two matrilineal moieties and three patrilineal trisections such as that of Ranon in the New Hebrides, while those in the direct male line of descent return to the same kinship section every two generations so that a man calls his father's father and sons' sons "brother", those in the direct female line of descent take three generations to complete the cycle so that it is the mother's mother's mother and for a woman her daughter's daughter's daughters who in this case are called "sister" (see Fig. 3).

Similarly, in a 12-section system such as that found in the Chou period in China, which is based on two patrilineal moieties and six matrilineal descent groups, the cycle takes 6 generations to repeat itself in the direct male line in such a way that it is the son's son's son's son's son's son's sons who fall into the category of "brothers". Thus each such "closed" kinship system, returning upon itself every so many generations, assumes the configuration of a human *mandala* divided into 4, 6, 8 or 12 sections, one of which is figured here and yet others are to be found depicted in Chapters V and VI of the above-mentioned work.

So far as is known, the 12-section system forms the uttermost limit to which such "closed" or "circular" kinship systems have been developed, and, by the time this stage is reached, the manifest object of the incest taboo in expanding society having been thus achieved[11], it falls to pieces and subsequently the very size of society itself, with its numerous opportunities, assures varied contact to such an extent that all these complicated taboos are no longer necessary and there remains among us today only the basic one prohibiting marriage with members of the biological family unit.

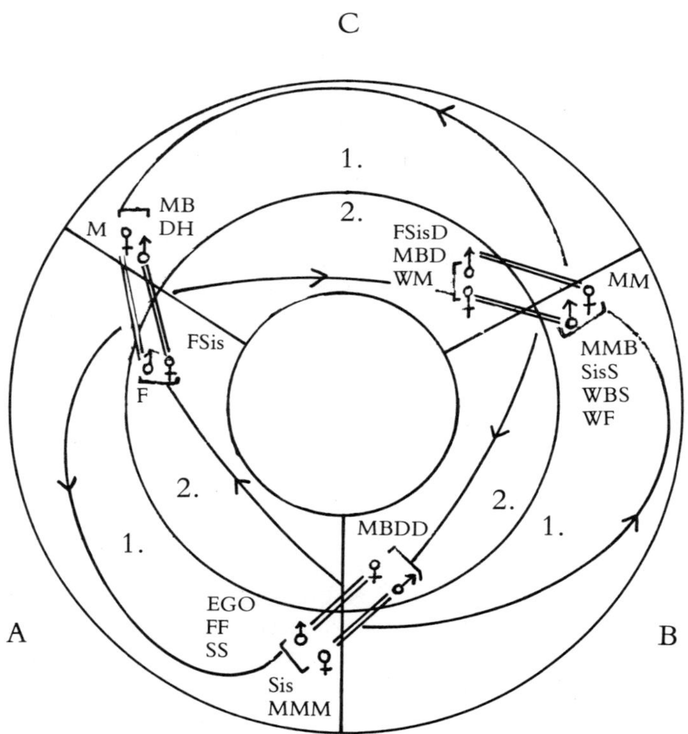

Fig. 3.
6-Section System. Functional Diagram ♂ = MBDD.
Matrilineal moieties represented by circular bands 1 and 2.
Radial lines divide the three patrilineal trisections A, B and C.
(From *Stone Men of Malekula*, Fig. 27, with kind permission of Messrs. Chatto and Windus.)

This diagram depicts the kinship system of Ranon in the island of Ambrim situated in the New Hebrides archipelago of Melanesia, where each man marries his mother's brother's daughter's daughter. This system repeats itself every 2 generations in the male line and every 3 generations in the female line, so that a man calls his father's father "brother" and his mother's mother's mother "sister".

3.
Latent or Inner Purpose of the Taboo: The Realisation of the "*Anima* Within"

Having now traced the external development of the *anima*-problem, for such it is, with its fulfillment in terms of mating with an actual spouse, what now of its inner development which must be of a complementary opposite nature, for, as the sexual desire towards the mother or sister recedes from consciousness, so must it inevitably increase as a psychological or spiritual longing.

I take it as axiomatic – and this lies I think at the root of all religion – that *every instinctive desire must ultimately be satisfied*, and that *what therefore cannot be satisfied in the flesh must be satisfied in the spirit*. This is where the whole Freudian rejection of spiritual values breaks down. Freud is honest enough, on page 247 of his *Totem and Taboo*, after his exposition of the Oedipus Complex and the consequent rise of male deities, to say: "In this evolution I am at a loss to indicate the place of the great maternal deities, who perhaps everywhere precede the paternal deities". This, I submit, is where Analytical Psychology comes in, and where true religion of a properly balanced kind comes in also. For, in the life of the individual, the incest taboo produces the following results. In the first place it forces the external search for the fulfillment of the mating instinct to reach out beyond its primary object within the biological family unit towards a more distant object with a view to enlarging the social and experiential horizon. But the repressed primary (incestuous) longings still exist, so that to the desire for the new mate is also added the disappointment that she is not all that is desired. And thus the second factor arises, namely that of the *projection of the unfulfilled part of the desire*, which acquires a negative and a positive aspect, of which the negative is always the first to become apparent, since, as in the case of the movement from a 4-section towards an 8-section system described above, it is the dissatisfaction which is always the spur to effort.

Thus we get, on the one hand, the negative attitude towards women and their consequent degradation in the social scale that is so characteristic of early patrilineal societies, coupled in the mythological sphere with the belief in a Devouring Earth Mother who, outraged by the treatment meted out to her sex, spends her time demanding blood-sacrifices of all kinds[12].

On the other hand we get the positive aspect of *fulfillment* on the religious level in three ways: firstly in those "sacred orgies" to which Freud refers "in which persons of just these forbidden degrees of kinship seek sexual union" (*Totem and Taboo*, page 18), thus demonstrating once more that biological in-breeding is *not* the purpose of the incest taboo; secondly in the almost universal belief at this cultural level that gods and culture-heroes in fact do just what men under normal circumstances are so cruelly forbidden to do, that is to say, break every incest taboo and mate with their mothers or sisters; and thirdly in the emergence of divine kings whose duty (as in Egypt and elsewhere) it was to marry their sisters.

In this way the primary desire is fulfilled either by men themselves when under special religious license to do so, that is when they themselves perform the "sacred marriage", or else in phantasy when the desire for this sacred incestuous marriage is projected upon the gods. It is to be noted, however, that even among the gods and culture-heroes the union is rarely with the most primary object of all, which is the mother, but more usually with the sister who is herself secondary to the mother.

These unions are as a rule accompanied by miraculous or unusual events all of which are highly symbolical, as when Erets, culture-hero of the small island of Atchin in the New Hebrides where I have worked, courted his sister Le-rets (note the similarity of name) by floating a kite over the channel which divided their habitations until it reached her house (where she was of course married in the flesh to another man), and to the kite he had attached a fowl which, by its crowing, made her look up and receive the message. The channel actually exists, but is, of course, symbolic of the division between the spiritual and material worlds. Birds everywhere signify spirit, and rope or string (in this case holding the kite) always signifies the union of conscious with unconscious, in other words, the sure but thin thread of spiritual intuition. The cock, as everyone knows, signifies the dawn, in other words, the gateway into the unconscious, its crowing being the signal announcing the passage from one sphere into the other, like that of the cock which crew three times during the Passion.

Internalisation through Sacrifice. The Psychology of Celibacy.

We have seen how the *social or manifest* purpose of the incest taboo is to enlarge the social horizon. We now see how its *latent or spiritual* purpose is to enlarge the spiritual horizon by developing the idea that there is after all a sphere in which the primary desire may be satisfied, namely the divine sphere of the gods together with that of their semi-divine counterparts, the culture-heroes.

This is however not all, for these are mythological projections, and, satisfying as they may be on this level, they do not achieve for man the ultimate spiritual union. This can be done only by sacrifice. The incest taboo is itself a sacrifice, but by no means a complete one, since the manifest purpose of the taboo is social only, and its spiritual aspect is not yet realised. The latent purpose of it on the spiritual level is achieved fully only when the taboo has been pushed to its uttermost and includes all women, that is to say with the advent of celibacy as a definite technique by means of which union with the divine can be achieved.

This raises the problem of celibate priests who come for psychological treatment because, for reasons unknown to them, they are inhibited in the conduct of their religious duties. It might by some be wrongly supposed that, when it came to the sexual aspect of their problems, ordinary analytical methods might be inapplicable to them on account of their ideal of celibacy and its enforcement by an authoritarian system. Experience shows, however, that psychological concepts regarding the release of libidinous matter not only apply to them quite as much as to the ordinary layman, but are applicable if possible even more, since true celibacy, far from being an affair of sex-repression, is itself, if rightly understood, the most complete expression of the transformed sex instinct. It is in fact the case that sex-repression in any form hinders the celibate even more than it hinders the married man. For what the celibate is seeking is deeper than sex, that is to say a direct union with "the other" which is God. But, since he is human and endowed with sex instinct without which he would be as nothing, and since individuation of any kind demands the fullest development of all desire, if sex desire is repressed the way to God is to that extent blocked also, and cannot be found until the unconscious inhibition is removed. This is so vital to the priesthood that it is astonishing how frequently it is overlooked. But the analysis of priests shows that it is the case, and that the sex instinct, far from being feared, has actually to be heightened to such a pitch that it bursts through the barriers of flesh and reaches the depths – or heights – which give access to the divine, bringing about a union formed not of flesh but of the spirit. And thus the incest taboo reaches its final goal, which is the *anima* within, divested of all projection in the form of fleshly desire upon the *anima* without.

Thus, to those not acquainted with monasticism, it comes sometimes as a surprise to learn that the monks' chief search was love, and that for example St. Bernard, the greatest of all Cistercians (who shut themselves off from the world and maintain the rule of almost complete silence), when addressing his monks as abbot used as his main text the Song of Songs, which is the most outstandingly sexual poem in Holy Writ. All mystical literature also is based on sexual imagery such as the Church being the Bride, and Christ the Bridegroom.

But, unlike the pagan gods and culture-heroes who married their sisters, Christ had no sister. He only had a Mother, and in the cult of and mystical union with Our Lady which is so intimately bound up with all monastic life the incestuous cycle becomes complete, since we are Christ's mystical body and the Mother is the first (though not the ultimate) object of our desire, the fulfillment of which, as it is our duty to avoid in the flesh so it is our soul's health to seek in the spirit.

Thus our following-out of the implications of the incest taboo has led us along the same road as the biblical one, which starts with Eve being born out of Adam's side, that is to say the creation of desire and of the *anima*-image. So long as Adam and Eve obeyed God in Eden there was no trouble, but there were also no children and no contact with the world outside. That is to say that they were "innocent", a state only possible within the womb and so long as mother and son are one. Man and the great Earth Mother were yet unseparated. As Isaiah, foretelling the return to this blissful state says in chapter 62, verses 4–5, "Thy land shall be married. For as a young man marrieth a virgin, so shall thy sons marry thee". The meaning of virginity will be returned to shortly. What is of importance here is the spiritual union between son and mother, which is the beginning and the end of the *anima* problem. But Eve rebelled, and she and Adam were cast out. That is to say that mankind as we know it was born. The divine and innocent incestuous union was broken. Henceforth Adam could not find his *anima* within himself, but had to seek her externally in the form of a wife. Now children came. Eve became "the mother of all living", but at the same time she had to suffer. And she suffered not only through the labour of childbirth – "in sorrow shalt thou bring forth children" – but also through the negative projections of Adam, who had followed her advice in seeking to put himself on a level with God, and through it had found himself cast out of Paradise. This may be equated with the age of the inferior status of women and the rise of the Devouring Goddesses. Adam's desire was towards Eve, but she disappointed him, and the desire being the will, we get that devastating picture of thwarted desire painted by St. Bernard in the passage quoted at the beginning of this essay, ending with "the will is thy Eve", the negative *anima* at its worst.

Then comes the revelation of the solution, Mary the Second Eve, who is the mother of the Second Adam, our Lord, who is Himself at the same time, in the tradition of the Church, her Spouse. But this time the mother was a Virgin, not the "mother of all living" as was Eve, but the mother of Him who Died. What is, then, the psychological meaning of Virginity?

4. Virginity

Virginity as spiritual pregnancy

Much has been written on this subject, and most readers of this essay will be familiar with Esther Harding's work on *Woman's Mysteries*[13] during the course of which she demonstrates the psychological meaning of "virginity" as symbolising a re-creative submission to the demands of instinct. There is no space in an essay of this size to do more than call attention to this remarkable work. To quote at length from the innumerable instances of Virgin Goddesses of Fertility which she cites in support of this thesis would be redundant, since they can be read in her book. So, since the plan of this essay is the much simpler one of tracing the history of the incest taboo in terms of the transformation of instinctive values into spiritual ones with reference first to the anthropological data and then to the traditional contrast between Eve and Mary, I propose not to weary the reader by quoting directly from her in the text. Instead, I will proceed along the lines previously laid down in this essay – which are largely based on the results of clinical observations – and end up with an account of two dreams illustrating what has been said, confining myself to making a few relevant quotations from her book in footnotes in order to show, in certain places where our subject-matter coincides, the striking similarity between the conclusions we both have reached.

In the first place, though we now think of the word "virgin" as being synonymous with "chaste", this was not the case either with the Greek word *parthenos* or with the Hebrew *almah* of which "virgin" is the most usual biblical translation. For the Greek word was used of an unmarried girl whether she was chaste or not, and was in fact also applied to unmarried mothers. The Hebrew word means likewise "unmarried" without reference to premarital chastity. Thus in both cases the criterion for judging whether a woman were what is translated "virgin" or not was not whether she was chaste or unchaste (which is a biological criterion) but whether she were unmarried or married (which is on the contrary a purely legal one)[14]. The dividing line was thus not one having to do with nature (which is divine, having been created by God) but with law (which is not divine, having been created by man).

This would appear at first sight to present us with an insoluble paradox, particularly because it is of the essence of Christianity to consider Our Lady chaste. This was, however, also the belief in classical and pre-classical times with regard to other mothers of divine heroes, though in these cases the "virginity" carried with it the supposition that the mother had been impregnated by a god. Similarly, Our Lady is said to have "conceived by the Holy Ghost". It is, however, not by chance that she conceived before she married for, as we have seen, what the ancients meant by the words which we translate "virginity" was not chastity but the absence of legal marriage. Indeed, it would appear that to be a virgin in the mythological sense the woman must conceive outside or before the marriage bond. Thus, had Our Lady been married at the time when she conceived she would no longer have been a virgin, and virginity is an essential attribute of the Mother of God[15].

What then do we mean by "virgin"? It may help us to examine those ways in which we use the word which are not directly concerned with sex. We speak of a "virgin forest" as being one in which the powers of nature are untrammeled and untouched by man. But we can think of this from two diamètrically opposite points of view. We can think of it either from the view of the agricultural pioneer, who would regard it as something to be destroyed and uprooted as soon as possible; or else we can think of it from the point of view of a nature lover who would regard the virgin forest with awe as a supreme manifestation of pregnant nature, and who would oppose all the most enlightened efforts of the agriculturalist or town-builder to destroy its primitive beauty – who would, in fact, treat it as inviolably holy. The one would represent "law and order" and the other "nature". So that we have here two opposite principles, both valid, the law of man in apparently open conflict with the law of God. Yet it is the law of God, the untrammeled law of pregnant though as yet chaotic nature that we dub "virgin", and it is the reduction of that chaos which we call Law and Order.

Thus in this sense the word "virgin" does not mean chastity but the reverse, the pregnancy of nature, free and uncontrolled, corresponding on the human plane to unmarried love, in contrast to controlled nature corresponding to married love, despite the fact that from the legal point of view sexual intercourse within the marriage bond is the only kind which is regarded as "chaste"[16].

It will be seen that this argument has landed us in the midst of a paradox, a paradox only to be solved either a) by regarding the whole biblical story of the Virgin Birth as purely allegorical, which the Church asserts it is not, it being, as she maintains, a unique historical event; or else b) by reconciling the two through the realisation that *instinct wants to be transformed into spirit*, and that the Virgin Birth is the supreme example of this having been achieved, as Our Lady's womanhood was so complete and so closely united with God that it became self-reproductive.

For what woman, in her inmost soul, would not like to give birth to a man child without all the bother of having a husband, a child with whom she might be in complete unity of spirit without any outside interference? Many married women in fact do reach out towards this solution, but in a condition of negative *participation mystique* due to a largely unconscious relationship with the husband owing to a mixture of fear and pride, leading to a spiritually incestuous relationship with the son. But the archetypal conception of Mary is, on the contrary, that she was so humbly receptive in herself that she was a fitting mate for the All Highest in the form of the Holy Ghost. That is to say that she was so virginal (*i.e.* uncontaminated by man's misconceptions) as to be worthy of this honour and of receiving of the heavenly spiritual semen direct without its having to pass through the body of an imperfect man.

For all man-made law is negative. The laws of marriage can never create children; they can, if observed, only prevent children from being born in an undesired way. The positive factor is instinct, and the negative factor of law acts as an inhibition against untrammeled instinct for the sake of coupling with it spiritual values.

This brings us back to the whole question of the repression *versus* the transformation of sex. Women who have repressed their sex do often in fact become barren. Such is the case often in America today and to a lesser extent in Western Europe. Women in some parts of Southern India have a remedy for this which is "miraculous" in the same sense as, though in a lesser degree than, the Virgin Birth. For here the creator god Shiva is represented in his temples by a stone phallus called *lingam* standing in a stone basin, which is a female symbol, thus representing the divine union; a divine union, be it noted, not on the biological level (for a phallus is not made of flesh) but on the spiritual. If a married woman, though having concourse with her husband, remains barren, she has recourse not to aphrodisiacs but to the male principle in the spirit (the *animus* as we should call it) and, rubbing her private parts on the stone *lingam*, goes back to her husband and conceives. This is because at least a certain modicum of spiritual union with the husband is necessary to supplement the biological union if pregnancy is to result. Similar results are achieved in Europe today by the psychological process of rescuing the woman's positive *animus* from the depths of the personal unconscious into which it has often sunk.

Our Lady similarly but on a yet deeper level worshipped and abased herself before the Lord to such an extent that her virginity, that is to say her spiritual pregnancy, blossomed also into a biological one in which spirit and matter were united in the Person of Christ. "Ever-Virgin" therefore means "Ever-Pregnant". And this Virgin Woman gave birth to the Virgin Son who himself is not only ever-pregnant through the working of the Holy Spirit, but also, in Church tradition, became her Spouse, fulfilling thus within the hearts of men not just the secondary sacred marriage with the Sister as so many pre-Christian culture-heroes do, but the primary union with the Mother who is on this spiritual level the ultimate goal.

Thus the incest taboo leads in full circle out of the biological sphere into the spiritual. This circle is well typified in the two incidents of the Gospel story as related by St. John, the first being at the outset of our Lord's career when he said to Mary, "Woman, what have I to do with thee?" (John 2, 4), and the second when on the Cross he committed her into the charge of the beloved disciple, saying "Behold thy Mother" (John 19, 27). Of these two utterances the first, spoken in connection with Christ's first miracle of turning the water into wine at the marriage in Cana, represents the taboo against union with the actual mother; whilst the second represents the consummation of this union not in the flesh but in the spirit. The "beloved disciple", held to have been John who was also a celibate and represents therefore the mystical body, is here mystically united with the Virgin Mother who henceforth becomes the positive mother-*anima*-image of Christendom.

Thus Mary at Cana represents the First Eve, the externalised mother archetype who is rejected, or "sacrificed" from the point of view of external human standards, and the same Mary during the Crucifixion, who at that instant finally gives up her Son, becomes fulfilled in that she becomes "the Mother of all living", the internalised mother-archetype in a new spiritual and mystic sense.

To sum up the point which we have now reached, the Garden of Eden represents the uncontaminated womb in which Adam and his *anima*, the First Eve, live in god-like communion. Then comes the Fall, when God speaks with two voices, firstly as "God" forbidding the eating of the one fruit which would make men "as gods", and secondly with the voice of the serpent telling man that he should eat it. The earthy nature of the serpent clearly corresponds to the earthy nature which Christ took on at the Incarnation when he "Who knew no sin" was "made to be sin on our behalf" (R. V. 2. Cor. 5, 21). It will be remembered that when in the desert men grumbled and were bitten by fiery serpents the Lord commanded Moses, "Make thee a fiery serpent, and set it upon a pole: and it shall come to pass, that every one that is bitten, when he looketh upon it, shall live" (Numbers 21, 8), and this brazen serpent has always been taken to be a type of Christ, the conscious Saviour who heals the complementary unconscious ill. So that the Fall came to be looked on as a *felix culpa*, or "fortunate sin" that dragged man out of his state of unconscious participation with the divine, causing him to pass through the vale of tears called "projection" in order finally to force him, if he is not to destroy himself, into internalising the mother-archetype in the form of a conscious redirection of will-power towards the *anima* within.

Seen from this standpoint the incest taboo is not therefore just a negative prohibition, but is a positive command to seek the kingdom of heaven not in the marriage of the flesh but in the marriage within. And this is why priests have to carry the taboo to its uttermost limits and remain celibate, because it is almost if not quite impossible to achieve both kinds of marriage at once, and the ideal at least of internal marriage has to be upheld even for the married to reach out to so far as they can[17].

Virginity as the "magic circle" of individuation.

So much from the point of view of the man. As to that of the woman, I propose first to make one short quotation from St. Bernard, and then quote the dream of a woman which first opened my eyes to the meaning of the virginity problem. St. Bernard is talking to monks, but what he says is of such universal application that it will be as good an introduction as any. In the same sermon on *Conversion* from which I have already quoted he says: "Thou hast sinned; cease from sinning . . . long has the overflowing cesspit been poisoning the whole house with its intolerable stench; vain is it for thee while still the filth flows in to pump it out, to repent while as yet thou dost not cease to sin . . . . *Shut the windows, watch the approaches, bar the openings with care*[18]; and so at last, when no fresh filth comes in, thou wilt be able to purge out the old"[19]. Then, after proceeding along the lines already quoted, he goes on to describe the soul when it has been thus purged, saying, "*It is an enclosed garden where a sealed fountain derives into four heads* and from one vein of wisdom fourfold virtue flows . . . . There the ointment of the spouse yields its most fragrant odour and the rest of sweet smells pervade when the north wind has fled and the south wind blows gently. There in the midst is the tree of life, that apple-tree of the Song of Songs, more precious than all the trees of the wood, whose shadow refreshes the spouse and whose fruit is sweet to her taste. There shines the fair beauty of continence and the vision of pure truth irradiates the heart's eyes; moreover to the ears the most sweet voice of the inward consoler brings joy and gladness"[20].

In the true style of the Fathers of the Church he packs into this brief passage quotations from Genesis, the Song of Songs and the Psalms, treating the whole Bible as a spiral structure in which the same themes occur almost endlessly on different levels and in varying contexts. But what interests us here is the concept of the *magic circle that must be closed* in order that the union with the spouse may be consummated, as also the fact that this magic circle is the same in the beginning as at the end, with the four rivers of Eden representing for us the four psychological functions, and the Tree of Life figuring, as in Apocalypse, in the New Jerusalem as well as in the Old.

This magic circle is at one and the same time the womb, the mother and the inviolate soul. The breaking of it lets in the "filth" and the sealing of it brings salvation.

Dreams demonstrating the inner meaning of Virginity as Pregnant Womanhood (with special reference to four ancestresses of Christ).

I will now end this paper by citing the case of a very vital woman who came into analysis because the man she was living with had become impotent. Or rather, he came into analysis first, but she quickly followed as soon as it became evident that the fault was not only his but was one arising out of their relationship and therefore coming from both sides. Part of her trouble was that she suffered from an extreme split in her *animus*-image, as a result of which she had come to divide men into two categories. One category was composed of "dark" fascinating intellectual men whose talk was both inspiring to listen to and who also, as she said, always brought out the best in her so that with them she also shone with intellectual brilliance, but who, for some unaccountable reason, always "let her down". The other category comprised what she described as "fair" men, who were slow, lacking in fire, dull, listless, stupid and not at all successful by worldly standards – indeed not by any standards at all, since they had neither push nor determination to get on in life, and no real sexual attraction. Yet it was to one of the latter category, after having been "let down" by a "dark" man, she had fled, and had lived with for the two years preceding the analysis while at the same time constantly complaining at his faithful dullness.

Her first act before coming into analysis was to try "scribbling", and what she felt to be the most meaningful of her scribblings was an impulsively drawn circle about 3 inches in diameter which was incomplete at the bottom left-hand corner, towards which breach, on the outside, she depicted, as if crawling, a small lithe snake-like form. This was quite evidently the point at which her psyche "leaked", both letting out what should be internalised psychic contents and at the same time admitting on the rebound the evil influence, the snake obviously being the sign of intellectual contamination (a mixture of fear and pride) which was ever on the look-out to destroy the virgin integrity of her soul. This incomplete circle threatened by the snake, occupying the right hand or conscious part of her sheet of paper, corresponded with the exciting desires towards the "dark" man. But this configuration was balanced by the presence, on the left upper side of the paper, of a kind of sluggish dragon-like creature of quite uncertain sex, depicting equally clearly the (to her) dull and uneventful union with the "fair" man which she at present had, but from which nevertheless she was unable to extricate herself precisely because the motivation for it was, to her, unconscious, and the only reason she could vocally give for continuing it was that, as she said, it was at least "safe".

The safety was, of course, one of stagnation, just as the danger of the other was the extremity of passion.

The problem was how to transform both these negative unions in the unconscious by uniting them into a single positive union in the conscious. For both conditions depicted in the "scribbling" were conditions of extreme *participation mystique*, that with her present partner who belonged to the "dull, fair" type, being manifestly inactive in the conscious though intensely active in the unconscious, whereas her previous connection with the "exciting, dark" man was active in her conscious life but, as the event had proved, inactive or only negatively active in the unconscious.

That is to say that both types of union failed because of the "leakage", on the one hand a leakage of psychic contents into the external world causing, as Jung puts it, a "primitive identity of the ego with ourselves, in other words, a complete absence of relationship"[21] and a wholesale projection; and on the other hand that internal contamination of the virginal psyche due to the introjection into it of false notions which is the antecedent cause of all such external projections. In other words, in her case, though Adam and Eve had been ejected from the Garden of Eden, the Angel with the flaming sword had *not* taken up his place at the entrance, so that what should be divided (in the conscious, *i.e.* differentiated) was not, and what should not be divided (in the unconscious) was. In yet other words, with her the spiritual incest taboo had not come into operation and, like Lot's wife, in turning back towards the city of contamination (*i.e.* mother-fixation, which in the biblical story took the form of active homosexuality), her heart had indeed become turned to stone. For the one legitimate relationship of *participation mystique* is that existing between mother and child within the womb, corresponding to Adam and Eve within the Garden, and to purely biological mating before the incest taboo. All looking back is ultimately a search to re-establish this blissful union in the flesh, and all looking forward is the effort to establish it in the spirit.

What transpired in the analysis was that in remaining tied in a condition of *participation mystique* with the "dull, fair" man, the dreamer was, in fact, seeking to re-capture the infantile incestuous relationship with her father, and that he was in her similarly seeking to recapture his mother. And in both cases, as evidenced by the duration of their union, this unconscious consideration quite overrode the adult sexual mating instinct and had, in fact, nullified it by rendering him impotent, till such a time as the various factors in the situation could be sorted out.

As a matter of fact they later married and reared a family.

The line taken by the analyst was, "If this apparently dull, unsatisfying and on the surface negative union has gone on for so long, there must be something positive in it to keep it going at all". This led to a simultaneous analysis of both partners, each of whom after a certain stage started dreaming about prostitutes, he dreaming that he was searching for one, and she that she was herself becoming one.

The prostitute is the archetype of the free woman, the woman untrammeled by man's laws. For dreams are on this level the complementary opposite of life in the flesh. In external life she has to pay a price much heavier than that paid by the man, but in dreams she represents the bountiful earth-mother[22], uncontaminated by thinking, who offers good things to all men and who is to be had for the asking, though the asking involves toiling with the sweat of one's brow, to dig, harrow, manure, and plant the soil. She is, in fact, the ultimate *anima*, the temple priestess who marries the god and bestows her favours upon devout men[23], thus raising them also to semi-divine status. On this spiritual level she is also Our Lady, who showers her gifts freely upon all men and who is *profligate* (note the word) with her divine favours. In fact she is in the psyche the Virgin Unspotted, pregnant with the boundless pregnancy of nature, translated into this spiritual sphere.

Why else should it be that not only was Our Lord's mother both unmarried and called Virgin, but that every one of the other four women mentioned in Christ's genealogy[24] as given in the first chapter of St. Matthew should be of a character that the modern, and indeed also the ancient, conventional outlook would label as "immoral"? These four, selected not haphazardly, but evidently with deliberate intent and leaving out all the respectably married ancestresses like Sarah, were:

a) Tamar who, disguising herself as a common prostitute, seduced her father-in-law Judah.

b) Rahab, the most prominent professional harlot in the Old Testament, who, however, repented and is held up as a model of repentance in the Epistles.

c) Ruth who seduced her husband's kinsman Boaz.

d) Bath-sheba, "her that had been the wife of Urias", whom David abducted and whose husband he treacherously caused to be killed in battle but who nevertheless became the mother of Solomon.

St. Jerome, in his Commentary on Matthew, says: "This was so designed in order that He who had come for the sake of sinners might, being born of sinners, blot out the sins of all, because He came not now as a Judge, but as a Physician, to heal our diseases". This explanation, as those also put forward by St. Chrysostom and others, may be true on one level, but from the point of view from which this paper is written, the reason for the inclusion of these four women alone in this genealogy is that they are all "virgins" in the sense that they represent undifferentiated womanhood, contaminated indeed on the conscious level of man's laws (though in the Bible story these matters are later accommodated), but uncontaminated in the spiritual virginity or integrity which prompted their actions. Nor were they (with the exception of Rahab, whose motherhood is recorded only in the Matthew genealogy and the circumstances of which therefore we do not know) just repentant sinners who later made respectable marriages, but it was actually out of their "immoral" unions that the ancestral line of Christ as traced through Joseph arose.

A whole paper could be devoted to an analysis of the stories of these four women, and of their roles as representing respectively the four psychological functions of womanhood as symbolised by the four rivers of Eden of which Mary is the head. I have the manuscript of such a paper already written, but it cannot be included here, and I must now return to the dreams of the modern woman already mentioned, an understanding of which throws much light on the whole problem of spiritual virginity as symbolised in dreams by sexual freedom, dreams being, it must always be remembered, on this deep level the very opposite of external life.

I propose to discuss only two dreams, both dreamt at a critical period of the analysis, in the first of which the dreamer found herself going down into a large underground room like a restaurant, which she at first took to be a night club but later realised was a brothel with women sitting at tables and sailors coming in and out. First mildly interested at this, she suddenly became horrified when the duenna of the place flung her arms round her, gave her a smacking kiss, and said, "Dearie, you are one of us. You will never get away from here now". The horror was in the dream. When she woke up, being already partially analysed, she began to overcome her horror and look more objectively at the situation. "Underground" meant, of course, the unconscious, where things are apt to be the reverse of what they seem. A prostitute is, from the male point of view, a totally undifferentiated woman, just Woman, who will give him what he wants on this undifferentiated level. Since differentiation is a thing that belongs to the conscious which is symbolised by "above-ground", this undifferentiation in the unconscious means for a woman freedom from the trammels of ego-consciousness and therefore the discovery of her true self. Apart from personal associations which so often distort archetypal patterns – and there were none in this dream – sailors and airmen always represent Spirit, though each represents spirit of a different kind, like the waters above and below the firmament. Airmen represent the volatile, male "Holy Ghost" aspect of spirit, and sailors its ponderable, heavy or earthy aspect, which is just what this woman needed to counteract her over-intellectualised flights that often carried her quite beyond the bounds set by the reality of a situation, and that made real and lasting contacts with actual men impossible or at least extremely difficult.

There were, of course, far too many sailors in the dream, allowing much too much choice and freedom to escape from any one of them. But, for the stage she was at, the dream was a very positive one, and the duenna's greeting and statement that she would "never get away from here now" meant that the analytical process had well bitten in, and that she could no longer escape from really facing up to her problems; that, in fact, the ground for salvation was already there. The duenna indeed represented the positive earth mother.

The next dream is the really vital one for the thesis of this paper. She dreamt that she was to be a blood-donor, and for this purpose had gone into a large hall, at the end of which was a table at which stood or sat a lady doctor. The room was full of other prospective blood-donors, all of whom were friends whom the dreamer had known in external life. The lady doctor was one whom she had previously known also in real life, and whom she had not very much liked. What was her horror therefore when this lady doctor asked her in a loud voice so that all could hear: "Are you a virgin?" and went on "Because if you are not a virgin, you won't do. Your hole will be too big". The dreamer thought it, to say the least, a bit tactless on the part of the lady doctor to say this so loud, though in fact all her friends in the room knew all about her. So she had to admit that she was not. So far, the scene was at least comprehensible, but what was her amazement when the lady doctor added, "But these two will do. They are virgins", and pointed to two girls the dreamer had known in her youth, both of whom she had envied on account of the extreme ease of their relationship with men, whereas she herself had suffered from great inhibitions, and both of whom were now married and had children. Yet they were dubbed virgins and pronounced good as blood-donors, and she was not. With this puzzle in her mind she woke up.

The first question put to her was what the lady doctor had meant by saying that her hole would be too big, and what this could have to do with blood-donating. The latter part of the question she was unable to answer, but she said that the first part immediately called to her mind a picture of the "dark" lover's member penetrating her. This concept called vividly to mind her original "scribbling" of the incomplete circle threatened by the lithe snake-like object, and it immediately became clear what in this dream "virginity" meant. That it did not refer to physical virginity was clear from the fact that though none of the three were physically virgins, the two successfully married women, both of whom had produced children, were regarded as being "virgins", whereas she herself was not. What the dream meant was, on the contrary, that with the two married women thinking had not contaminated feeling; that is to say, "moral" values quite proper in themselves when confined to consciousness had not got loose from their proper sphere and penetrated into the unconscious where they become the reverse. In other words, these two women had not contaminated their fundamental womanhood and had maintained ease of relations both with their own souls and with men, and were therefore spiritually "pregnant virgins"; whereas the dreamer herself, through faulty upbringing and the psychological muddle in which her parents had lived, had "moral" values shoved down her throat too early and therefore *had* contaminated her soul by substituting thinking for feeling, and thus could *not* establish proper relations either with her soul or with men. And so the paradox comes about that the married mothers with children were spiritual virgins, but that she herself was not. The virginity of the dream has nothing to do with physical virginity but everything to do with that of the soul[25]. Virginity of the soul means uncontamination and therefore pregnancy of the soul leading to easy pregnancy of the body. But lack of virginity of the soul means lack of pregnancy both in soul and sometimes also in body, because lack of pregnancy (which means lack of spiritual "virginity") in the soul prevents satisfactory relationship with any man, and in her case had reacted upon the man she was now living with in such a way as to make him impotent too, though it could not have done so had he not had a similar contamination of feeling by thinking in his psychological make-up also.

This dream, of course, raises many other questions which there is no space to go into here. So I will confine myself to saying that the symbol of the "unclosed hole" occurs in a sexual context not only in women's dreams but also in men's. A man of thirty, suffering from extreme retarded development due to an over-masculine mother and over-feminine father, dreamt constantly that he penetrated his mother or mother-substitute and that when he withdrew the "hole" remained open. This meant that the magic circle of his inner integrity had never closed, that is to say that, though physically a virgin, his spiritual virginity had never been sufficiently established, and that he was ceaselessly open to the influence of the false thinking mechanisms of his mother, whom he hated but from whom at the same time he could never get really free. In other words, the psychological incest taboo had never been established with him either.

With this I must bring this overlong essay to a close, apologising both to Professor Jung and to the reader for the fact that, owing to war-time conditions, it has not proved possible to condense or work over it as closely as might otherwise have been the case.

It has been my object in it to establish the two-fold purpose of the incest taboo by first demonstrating its manifest content which is the expansion of society, and then indicating its complementary opposite latent content which is the fulfillment within the psyche of that which the taboo forbids us so stringently in the flesh, namely the union with the uncontaminated mother-principle represented by the spiritual return into the womb. The words of the *Salve Regina* addressed to the Virgin Mother, "and after this our exile, show us the blessed fruit of thy womb Jesus", describe the process better than any. For on this level the incest taboo is the exile, which cuts mankind off from the object of his most intense desire in order that, through exile from it in the flesh, he may rediscover it in the spirit and, having re-entered the womb, be born again.

1. The quotations are made from the English translation by Watkin Williams: *Of Conversion*, a sermon to the clergy by Saint Bernard of Clairvaux, translated by Watkin Williams, London, 1938.
2. Christ's so-called brothers are taken to be brothers in the classificatory sense only, as described in endnote 7.
3. Sigmund Freud, *Totem and Taboo*, English translation by A.A. Brill, London, 1919.
4. John Layard, *Stone Men of Malekula*, London, 1942, pp. 102, 115 ff., 593.
5. See page 160 of this article.
6. Freud, *Totem and Taboo,* p. 14
7. John Layard, *Stone Men of Malekula*, p. 103. With regard to this and other marriages with specific relatives mentioned in this article, it may be objected that such a relative might not exist. As explained in detail on p. 99 of that work, however, almost all primitive kinship systems are organised on a so-called "classificatory" principle by means of which certain collateral relatives are classed together in such a way that, for example, in an overtly matrilineal community the mother's sister's son is for sociological purposes called "brother". If, then, a man's mother has no brother with a suitable daughter for him to marry, one of her classificatory brothers will provide his daughter instead.
8. A. M. Hocart, *Kings and Councillors*, Cairo, 1936, pp. 273-277.
9. For a more detailed exposition of this, see my *Stone Men of Malekula*, p. 116.
10. *Ibid*. p. 151.
11. In other parts of the world the expansion is achieved by unilateral methods, whether matrilineal or patrilineal, or else by a mixture of both in varying degrees.
12. A brief discussion of the Female Devouring Monster as compensating in the unconscious for the inferior position given to woman in the conscious will be found in *Stone Men of Malekula,* pp. 219 ff.
13. M. Esther Harding, *Woman's Mysteries, ancient and modern*, Longmans Green, first English edition, London, 1935.
14. Compare Harding, *op. cit.*, pp. 76 and 79, in which she describes the real meaning of "virgin" as contrasting with "married". The Latin *virgo* similarly meant simply "unmarried" without reference to chastity, as is shown by the phrase *virgo intacta* used for a chaste woman.
15. See Harding, *op. cit.*, p. 76, referring to pre-Christian times in which the Great Mother was always a "Virgin".
16. See Harding, *op. cit.*, p. 76, quoting Frazer's remarks on Artemis as "a goddess of fertility though not of wedlock" and on "her constant identification with the unmarried but not chaste Asiatic goddesses of fertility"; and p. 77 regarding Ishtar as "not the exclusive wife of any male god" but "nevertheless referred to constantly as the Virgin"; also p. 78 with references to Aphrodite as "virgin", Demeter "who execrated marriage", and many others.
17. See Harding, *op. cit.*, p. 271, quoting Philo of Alexandria: "For the congress of men for the procreation of children makes virgins women. But when God begins to associate with the soul, he brings to pass that she who was formerly woman becomes virgin again"; also p. 275 regarding the nun's union with God.
18. My italics.
19. *De Conversione*, p. 13.
20. *De Conversione*, p. 35.

21. C. G. Jung, *Contributions to Analytical Psychology*, London, 1928, p. 190.
22. See Harding, *op. cit.*, p. 78, on the subject of Ishtar being referred to as "The Prostitute", and of the Chinese Holy Virgin who bore a son while yet a virgin and is patroness of prostitutes; also p. 94, on which she quotes from a Roman Catholic book on the Saints the legend of how Mary the Gipsy or the Egyptian, whose face was black, "wishing to go to the Holy Land on a pilgrimage was to offer herself as a prostitute to the sailors on a vessel bound for that shore".
23. See Harding, *op. cit.*, pp. 268-70 regarding the *hieros gamos*, saying that "for the woman the significance of the experience must have been in her submission to instinct".
24. This is, of course, the genealogy of Christ as traced through Joseph, which would appear to deny Virgin Birth. Luke (Chapter 3) has a much longer one leading back to Adam, who is there called "the son of God". The Matthew genealogy goes back only to David, and is designed to show Christ's royal lineage. Both gospel writers notice the discrepancy regarding the Virgin Birth, Matthew by simply referring to Joseph as "the husband of Mary", and Luke by saying that Christ was Joseph's son, "as was supposed". The inference is either that, if Joseph was not in fact his father, Mary was also of the same lineage and that the two might be first cousins (as were Mary and Elizabeth), in which case their marriage would be in line with that of Jacob and Rachel; or else simply that Christ, being adopted by Joseph, would in law be reckoned to be his son. In either case the genealogy, placed thus in the forefront of the New Testament, cannot be due to chance but must be of deep psychological import.
25. This is what Esther Harding means by her constant references to a woman being "one-in-herself" (*op. cit.*, p. 80 and elsewhere).

Index

INDEX

INDEX

INDEX

INDEX

INDEX

INDEX

INDEX

INDEX

INDEX

INDEX

INDEX

INDEX